Dr. James Gills has written an instru pelling summary of the most foundational principle of the Christian life: *Resting in His Redemption*. This is the way we must begin and grow in the Christian life. God's grace brings forgiveness to us and enables us to face and fulfill the difficult challenge of forgiving others who hurt us deeply.

Perhaps even more difficult is the necessity to receive God's grace to live free from condemnation. We must abandon ourselves to His grace, His love, and His redemption. This is the only way to find the peace that flows from resting in His redemption. I recommend this book to all who want to know the Lord and who want to grow in the grace and knowledge of our Lord Jesus Christ.

—R. T. KENDALL
AUTHOR, *TOTAL FORGIVENESS*

The secret of experiencing contentment is not financial security, personal popularity, political authority, or anything else that so many people strive for today. Contentment is God's gift to the redeemed. Dr. Jim Gills, a personal friend who has been a source of great blessing in our lives, gives a road map for inner peace in *Resting in His Redemption*.

—DAN AND ANNE GRAHAM LOTZ

Dr. Jim Gills has written a superb book that is an excellent summary of the Bible from beginning to end—rest in His redemption. Count me a Jim Gills enthusiast.

—CHUCK COLSON, FOUNDER
PRISON FELLOWSHIP AND CHUCK COLSON CENTER
FOR CHRISTIAN WORLDVIEW

As I read this manuscript, my heart was warmed and edified. I was also mentally stampeded as I thought of those dear people, beginning with my own family members, who truly need to read this book. *Resting in His Redemption* is a must-read for spiritually sensitive, hungry, and seeking people everywhere!

—Pastor Dick Woodward
Founder and Teacher, Mini Bible College

In *Resting in His Redemption*, Dr. Gills's emphasis is how to live our daily lives resting in Christ's redemptive work. The Scriptures from beginning to end scream out the truth of our *resting in His redemption*, so clearly outlined in this magnificent manuscript. I agree that it is a must-read for all believers and sincere seekers of Jesus Christ.

—Dois I. Rosser, Jr.
Chair and Founder, International Cooperating
Ministries (ICM)

I have known Dr. Jim Gills for over thirty-five years. I was delighted to receive his latest manuscript before publication. As a corneal transplant surgeon, I have worked with him on a daily basis for over nine years. He rarely leaves my presence without whispering in prayer, "Rest in His redemption." His latest book exemplifies the grace, rest, and spiritual strength that Jim brings to a busy ophthalmology practice on a daily basis. It is the denouement of his lifetime of searching after God, which he is now sharing with us through his writing.

In this book is found the best of Dr. Gills; it will bless the reader, family, and friends of the Christian whose inflamed and resting heart radiates God's love and redemption.

—Jim Rowsey, MD

As a Catholic laywoman, I began serving in the ministry of healing and spiritual direction almost forty years ago, following the untimely death of a son. I know from experience that the only way to find peace and contentment in the midst of trials, suffering, and crisis is total surrender and abandonment to divine providence. *Resting in His Redemption* is the only answer to the turmoil people are facing in their lives today. This book is a *must,* not only for those seeking peace of mind and heart, but also for those desiring a deeper relationship with Christ, who is our only hope and our redemption.

—DIANE F. BROWN

I am personally deeply grateful for the simple but profound message that is so beautifully expressed in *Resting in His Redemption.* Coming from a Jewish culture that is so performance-oriented and competitive, I am awed and comforted in learning that Shabbat (the Sabbath) is not just a day of rest but a *lifestyle* that leads to an eternal divine romance.

—STEVEN L. SHERMAN
AUTHOR AND SPEAKER

There is something about human DNA that drives us to fulfill empty religious rules and ritual. It creates negative mind-sets, which our Lord Jesus Christ came to remedy, including guilt, shame, and failure. That's why Martin Luther said that we should preach the good news to each other lest we become discouraged. Dr. Gills has "preached the good news" in a way that makes me want to sing the "Hallelujah Chorus." What a wonderful book! Read it and then keep it in your library so you can read it at least once every year. This is a book that will keep you from being discouraged.

—STEVE BROWN
AUTHOR AND TEACHER

RESTING
IN HIS
REDEMPTION

RESTING
IN HIS
REDEMPTION

JAMES P. GILLS, MD

CHARISMA
HOUSE

Most CHARISMA HOUSE BOOK GROUP products are available at special quantity discounts for bulk purchase for sales promotions, premiums, fund-raising, and educational needs. For details, write Charisma House Book Group, 600 Rinehart Road, Lake Mary, Florida 32746, or telephone (407) 333-0600.

RESTING IN HIS REDEMPTION by James P. Gills, MD
Published by Charisma House
Charisma Media/Charisma House Book Group
600 Rinehart Road, Lake Mary, Florida 32746
www.charismahouse.com

Cover design by Nathan Morgan; Design Director: Bill Johnson

Visit the author's website at www.lovepress.com.

Library of Congress Cataloging-in-Publication Data:
Gills, James P., 1934-
   Resting in His redemption / James Gills. -- 1st ed.
       p. cm.
   Includes bibliographical references (p.   ).
   ISBN 978-1-61638-349-7 (trade paper) -- ISBN 978-1-61638-425-8
(e-book) 1. Contentment--Religious aspects--Christianity. 2.
Redemption--Christianity. I. Title.
   BV4647.C7G55 2011
   234'.3--dc22
                                        2011011413

15 16 17 18 19 — 9 8 7 6 5 4
Printed in the United States of America

DEDICATION

To the Mind, the Heart, and the Hands

CERTAIN INDIVIDUALS HAVE had an impact on my own faith in Christ, some through their writings and teachings, others more directly. I dedicate this volume to three special men.

First, to Oswald Chambers, whose classic writings focus on the Christian resting in God's redemption, His love, His grace, His mercy, and His person.

Second, to John Piper, for teaching us that God is most glorified in us when we are satisfied in Him.

Third, to Dois Rosser, who represents not only the mental awareness of Christianity but also the truly heartfelt excitement of living the Christian life; through his hands, Christ has been extended to thousands of others.

The mind of Oswald Chambers, the affections and excitement of John Piper, and the hands of Dois Rosser have demonstrated through their lives that they are resting in God's redemption. They reflect the beautiful fruit that comes from resting in the Redeemer's love.

CONTENTS

INTRODUCTION / 1

PART 1

The Biblical Basis for All Prayer Is Resting in His Redemption

1 Created for Communion With God / 15

2 Receiving God's Redemption / 43

PART 2

The Biblical Basis for All Christian Living Is Resting in His Redemption

3 Faith for Redemption / 59

4 Walking in God's Forgiveness / 99

PART 3

The Biblical Basis for Total Forgiveness Is Resting in His Redemption

5 Forgiving Others / 115

6 Freedom From Condemnation / 133

PART 4

The Biblical Basis for Divine Contentment Is Resting in His Redemption

7 Divine Contentment / 147

8 Cultivating an Eternal Focus / 175

NOTES / 201

INTRODUCTION

"WHAT IS THE chief end of man?" asks the Westminster Catechism. The answer: "Man's chief end is to glorify God, and to enjoy him forever." What does it mean to *glorify God? To enjoy Him—forever?* According to the catechism, "The Word of God, which is contained in the Scriptures of the Old and New Testaments, is the only rule to direct us how we may glorify and enjoy him."[1]

Indeed, the Scriptures teach clearly that God desires to live in intimate fellowship and communion with mankind. God is love (1 John 4:8), and He wants us to enjoy His love, peace, joy, companionship, and all of His divine attributes. He wants us to rest in His redemption, experiencing the perfect harmony and contentment and fulfillment of purpose for which He created us. The apostle Paul concluded that we should live in such a way "that we should be to the praise of his glory, who first trusted in Christ" (Eph. 1:12).

Did you know that God's original purpose for creating mankind was for us to enjoy covenant relationship with Him? How many Christians have understood this covenant of divine love, the desire of God's heart to live in communion and intimate companionship with them?

How many would say their priority in life is to enjoy God, experiencing His perfect harmony, peace, rest, and contentment available to them in that divine relationship? This is

1

the kind of fellowship that the first couple, Adam and Eve, enjoyed in the garden of Eden, when God walked with them in the cool of the evening (Gen. 3:8).

Then sin entered the human experience and separated all mankind from the bliss of that divine fellowship. But in the fullness of time, God sent His Son to atone for our sin. When we place our faith in Christ's sacrifice for our sin, we are redeemed by the blood of Christ and justified in the sight of God:

> Therefore, since we have been justified through faith, we have peace with God through our Lord Jesus Christ, through whom we have gained access by faith into this grace in which we now stand.
> —ROMANS 5:1–2, NIV

This peace and joy that come from resting in God's love and grace and an intimate relationship with our Creator-Redeemer are essential; they are the basic foundation of all the Judeo-Christian faith. All born-again believers have experienced that initial peace with God that their salvation brings. But that is not the end of the matter; it is only the beginning.

God's intention is that we be completely restored—spirit, soul, and body—to the divine rest found in His redemption. He wants us to experience the ever-unfolding mystery of intimate communion with our Creator-Redeemer.

Too often, as Christians, we try to prove our love for God through our works and personal efforts to be righteous. We focus on perfecting *our* love for God without learning to rest in *His* love for us. John, the beloved apostle, gives us the right order when he says that we love God because He first loved us (1 John 4:19). Without learning to rest in God's love for us, we cannot hope to truly love Him in return.

The message of the entire Bible can be summarized in this simple truth: *God created mankind for the purpose of knowing Him, loving Him, and enjoying intimate fellowship with Him.* The apostle Paul's poignant cry, "that I may know him, and the power of his resurrection" (Phil. 3:10), is a powerful witness to this truth.

Paul uttered this yearning plea for greater relationship with God late in life. It was long after his dramatic conversion, his great success in establishing many churches, and receiving wonderful revelation from God. In spite of all his success in the kingdom of God, Paul's burning desire was still, above all, *to know Christ intimately.*

The acceptance of Christ's sacrifice for our sin should birth in us a growing spiritual conviction in the heart that brings us into an ever deepening, personal, intimate relationship with God. Attending church regularly, reading the Bible occasionally, and giving mental assent to the truth that Christ died for our sin does not always motivate us to know Him with the passion Paul displayed. When we actually pursue the mystery of intimate relationship with God, we abandon ourselves to Him in our daily situations and He becomes the priority of our lives and our personal fulfillment. When we seek the Holy Spirit to dwell within us, He guides us into all truth (John 16:13). He reveals the wonderful mystery of resting in His redemption, of living in communion with Christ and finding His continual rest for our souls, regardless of our circumstances in life (Matt. 11:28).

In this book, we will discuss four important aspects of fulfilling the deepest desire of the human heart—to know God personally and intimately—in the way God's great, loving heart intended. To know the love of God that brings true heart contentment, we need to live life embracing these divine principles:

- Part 1: The biblical basis for all prayer is *resting in His redemption.*

- Part 2: The biblical basis for all Christian living is *resting in His redemption.*

- Part 3: The biblical basis for total forgiveness is *resting in His redemption.*

- Part 4: The biblical basis for divine contentment is *resting in His redemption.*

As you meditate on these biblical truths, your life will be transformed by the power of the Holy Spirit when you seek Him to make them a reality in your heart. The love of God for you that surpasses knowledge and the peace of God that passes understanding (Phil. 4:7) will fill your heart. You will become a victorious lover of the Lamb. Then you will glorify Him in all you do, enjoy God, and bring His love to all with whom you come into contact.

THE BASIS FOR ALL PRAYER

The biblical basis for all prayer is resting in His redemption. Oswald Chambers wrote: "We look upon prayer as a means of getting things for ourselves; the Bible idea of prayer is that *we may get to know God Himself.*"[2]

Chambers also taught that "prayer does not fit us for the greater work; prayer *is* the greater work."[3] The Christian life is *not* about working for Christ through your human toil, personal sacrifice, and disciplined intentions. The true Christian experience is expressed in knowing God intimately and resting in His redemption. Your entire motivation for prayer and for serving God is to be based on knowing Him, living in dependence on His loving grace, and becoming one with His purpose for your life.

THE BASIS FOR ALL CHRISTIAN LIVING

Enjoying the love, joy, peace, grace, and total redemption of your Creator-Redeemer is the basis for all Christian living. Your Christian life is validated by placing your faith totally in the power of Christ's redemption of your soul. As a believer, the simplicity of the gospel message is fulfilled in your learning to enter into a divine mystery of intimate relationship with God through prayer and communion with Him. Jesus taught us this principle of abiding in Him so that our lives will become exceedingly fruitful (John 15).

This abiding rest in Christ is *not* characterized by an absence of meaningful activity or by a lack of purpose. Rather, it is reflected in freedom from restlessness and discontentment that plague every human heart. Christians who have abandoned themselves to this divine rest, which is inherent in learning to abide in Christ, enjoy supernatural peace and joy even in life's most difficult challenges. Jesus invited all of us into this life:

> Come unto me, all ye that labour and are heavy laden, and I will give you rest. Take my yoke upon you, and learn of me; for I am meek and lowly in heart: and ye

shall find rest unto your souls. For my yoke is easy, and
my burden is light.

—MATTHEW 11:28–30

THE BASIS FOR TOTAL FORGIVENESS

There may be some who feel they have sinned too greatly to
receive the forgiveness of God and enter into this love relationship with Him. Their sense of personal guilt may cause them to
believe that they do not deserve to be forgiven by a holy God.
For those tormented souls, the Scriptures offer this liberating
promise: "But God commendeth his love toward us, in that,
while we were yet sinners, Christ died for us" (Rom. 5:8).

In the apex of your sinfulness, Christ made Himself a sacrifice to atone for your sin. The only condition for receiving
His forgiveness, regardless of the depravity of your sin, is
placing your faith in His sacrifice at Calvary. Though it seems
too good to be true, the entire New Testament confirms that
when you dare to come to Christ with deep spiritual conviction, He will set you free from sin and its guilt. Millions of
sinners who have experienced so great a salvation also confirm this divine truth.

Accepting God's total forgiveness

There are many people for whom the forgiveness of God
is a blessed reality. Having placed their faith in the sacrifice
of Christ for cleansing from sin, they have peace with God.
They have received His love and redemption for their sin. Yet
they cannot (or will not) accept *total forgiveness* for their
sinful past or even their present shortcomings. Their sense of
guilt for their own moral failures or for having hurt others

torments them every day of their lives, leaving them filled with self-condemnation.

That torment is not God's will for a born-again Christian. He wants to cleanse your heart and mind from all true guilt, as well as feelings of guilt, so that you can live in peace. Only then can you become fruitful in your Christian life. My friend R. T. Kendall explains, in his book *How to Forgive Ourselves Totally,* that we must accept God's total forgiveness for each sin that haunts us in order to be effective Christians and fulfill our God-given purpose.[4]

The Basis for Divine Contentment

It is the goal of our consumer-oriented culture to make you discontented with what you have, what you look like, or who you are. As a potential consumer, you must be made to feel discontentment in order to enhance the bottom line of various companies by investing in their product, service, or image. No wonder there is so little contentment in our culture.

Yet even those who are able to acquire all that is marketed as a potential means of personal contentment do not seem content. They simply do not reflect that happy state of mind that the Christian who discovers the mystery of contentment in God enjoys. For all their investments in toys, cruises, bank accounts, and other "guaranteed" sources of happiness, there seems to always be a drive to obtain more.

Jeremiah Burroughs (1599–1646), a member of the Westminster Assembly and a prolific writer, called Christian contentment "a box of precious ointment, very comfortable and useful for troubled hearts, in troubled times and conditions…a sweet, [inward] heart-thing, it is a work of the Spirit within doors."[5] He called contentment "the inward submission of the heart"[6] to the mystery of a divine romance with God.

Burroughs taught what would be considered a radical conclusion for our consumerism mentality: "Seeking to add a thing will not bring contentment. Instead, subtracting from your desires until you are satisfied only with Christ brings contentment."[7] Making relationship with Christ your first priority, as the apostle Paul reflected in his life, is the source of true contentment.

Being content in Christ, however, does not mean we are *satisfied* with our relationship with Him. With Paul, we continually cry out to know Him more. That is why a Christian can be the most contented person yet still unsatisfied.

Burroughs concludes that for a believer "a little in the world will content a Christian for his passage, but all the world, and ten times more, will not content a Christian for his portion…for there's the mystery of true contentment…that soul that is capable of God, can be filled with nothing else but God." In short, believers who find contentment in relationship with God have been ruined for lesser things; their lives have been consummated in the mystery of divine romance with their Lord. The only thing that will satisfy them is knowing God more intimately.

THE MYSTERY OF DIVINE ROMANCE

True Christianity is friendship with God. It is plunging into the divine river of His love, basking in the refreshing pool of His grace, drinking from the supernatural fountain of God's forgiveness, and receiving restoration of your soul.

We are called to enter into the mystery of Christ's love by learning to abide in Him continually. Jesus said, "Abide in me, and I in you. As the branch cannot bear fruit of itself, except it abide in the vine; no more can ye, except ye abide in me" (John 15:4). As a branch does not exist apart from the tree that formed it, so contentment in our Christian life is utterly dependent on the mystery of our being "in Christ."

It is in embracing the mystery of divine romance with Christ that our impassioned hearts will be motivated to fulfill our highest purpose in life. Focusing on His love, peace, and joy will transform every aspect of our lives—our personal holiness, our family and other relationships, our pursuit of work, and our recreation.

Why do we call it a *mystery*? Because as we learn to rest in His redemption, we experience a joy of divine relationship with our Savior beyond anything we can comprehend or explain.

Why do we refer to it as *romance*? Because there is no more profound way of explaining the divine fellowship of love we experience as we abide in the Person of Jesus Christ.

The apostle Paul described this intimate relationship with Christ throughout his epistles. He wrote: "Christ in you, the hope of glory" (Col. 1:27). And he prayed for believers that "Christ may dwell in [their] hearts by faith" and that "[they] might be filled with all the fulness of God" (Eph. 3:17, 19).

This divine romance involves living continually in intimate relationship and personal communion with God, who is our life. As we abide in His presence, we find the peace and joy that our hearts crave. In contrast, when we fail to make this divine relationship our priority, our life simply unravels and falls apart. We become restless and discontented, anxious and filled with foreboding.

Resting in His redemption is the consummation of the Christian life. It is really learning to live in the Person of Jesus, as the apostle Paul declared: "For in him we live, and move, and have our being" (Acts 17:28). As we abandon ourselves to God's love, we receive His grace, by faith, for the forgiveness of our sin. We also receive grace to forgive others and to accept total forgiveness for ourselves. And in learning to live in communion with Christ, we develop a powerful prayer life and enjoy divine contentment in fellowship with our Lord.

THE ESSENCE OF THE BIBLE MESSAGE

In its essence, the message of the entire Bible is that mankind was created for divine rest. We were not created with a need just for physical rest but for divinely ordained rest and harmony of spirit, soul, and body. This supernatural well-being of believers is taught throughout the Old and New Testaments. God spoke to His people through the prophet Isaiah:

> This is the true rest [the way to true comfort and happiness] that you shall give to the weary, and, This is [true] refreshing—yet they would not listen [to His teaching].
> —ISAIAH 28:12, AMP

You were made to live in intimate relationship with God the Father, God the Son, and God the Holy Spirit. The forgiveness available to every soul who comes to Christ in faith is the only true source that quiets the unrest of your humanity. Receiving the peace of God *will* transform your heart and mind so that you can be restored to a life of *resting in His redemption*.

Unfortunately, that has not been the daily experience of many Christians. They either have not understood or have not availed themselves of the true rest of the believer in Christ. Making relationship with God the priority of life and entering into intimate communion with Him is a journey, which not all believers have made the daily focus of their lives.

If you desire to experience more of God's rest, peace, and joy in communion with Him, I invite you to open your mind and heart to the message of this book. As you journey into the truth of the wondrous mystery of God's love for you, it may seem too good to be true. That is because the love of God is unlike anything this world has to offer. You will be ruined for any lesser, temporal pleasures or loves once you taste more deeply the divine wonder of *resting in His redemption.*

PERSONAL MEDITATION

What is the chief end of man, according to the Westminster Catechism?

_____

_____

Both Old and New Testaments teach that we should live in intimate communion with God. What separates us from God?

_____

_____

Why must all prayer be based on *resting in His redemption?*

_____

_____

Does the Lord actually *command* us to come to Him? (See Exodus 19:4 and Matthew 11:28.)

_____

_____

What is our godly covenant of relationship as a Christian?

_____

_____

What is divine rest?

_____

_____

PART 1

THE BIBLICAL BASIS FOR ALL PRAYER IS RESTING IN HIS REDEMPTION

We look upon prayer as a means of getting things for ourselves; the Bible idea of prayer is that we may get to know God Himself.

—OSWALD CHAMBERS[1]

I have been driven many times to my knees by the overwhelming conviction that I had absolutely no other place to go.

—Abraham Lincoln

Prayer...is a voice which goes into God's ear, and it lives as long as God's ear is open to holy pleas, as long as God's heart is alive to holy things. God shapes the world by prayer.... The mightiest successes that come to God's cause are created and carried on by prayer.

—E. M. Bounds[1]

1

CREATED FOR COMMUNION WITH GOD

I ONCE KNEW A wonderful gentleman who lived a long, peaceful life so filled with joy that all who knew him loved him. They sometimes expressed their wonder at the glow of peace and joy that radiated from him and the gorgeous smile that lit up his face when he greeted them. He had a way of making each person he saw feel special. Even in times of crisis, he reflected the peace of God in his demeanor and was obviously full of joy.

My friend was often asked why he seemed so happy. He would smile broadly and say that his communion with God was his source of happiness. When pressed to explain, he shared that throughout his life he made a practice of reading the Scriptures several hours a day and praying diligently in pursuit of an intimate relationship with His lovely Lord. He had learned that getting to know God was much sweeter than anything this natural life had to offer. And in turn, his communion with God made his life much sweeter.

He added that his continual fellowship with the Lord gave him a profound sense of belonging to God and of being deeply loved by Him. That divine love filled his heart with peace and joy. As a result, he lived his life sharing the love of God with others. He had learned to appreciate and value each person as God does. And in seeking God's heart, he escaped the temptations of worry, fear, anger, and other natural responses to our troubled world.

In stark contrast to my friend's exuberant joy, the wife of this godly man was constantly atwitter, worried about this, concerned about that. Her countenance did not reflect peace but anxiety and unrest. She was known to be critical of others, even fellow believers in Christ. Those who observed her understood her energies were consumed with trying to resolve her daily worries.

FOR HER, BEING A CHRISTIAN WAS MORE OF AN OUTWARD APPEARANCE.

This unhappy woman did not understand what scientific studies show: that most of what we worry about never materializes. Though she said she was a Christian, she lived as if she were solely responsible for life's every moment. She did not take time to pursue God as her husband did. She did not seek God's rest and joy for herself, though she was a constant witness to the fruit of that divine relationship in the demeanor of her husband. At the time of his death, they had been married sixty years. Yet his wife had never received the comfort her husband offered her or the love he wanted to share with her.

For her, being a Christian was more of an outward appearance. It was based on religious actions that belied her inner anxiety as she attempted to control her life. In her constant state of *unrest*, she never truly experienced the intimate love relationship with God that her husband enjoyed. As a result, she forfeited the comfort of communion with her husband as well as with her God.

Unfortunately, this negative, anxious behavior of my friend's wife seems common to many people, even professing Christians. They do not reflect the radiant peace, joy, and loving character displayed by my friend. In his constant pursuit of God, my friend had discovered the purpose for living: to totally abandon ourselves to Christ so that we reflect His character of love, joy, and peace.

Throughout his life, my friend gave of himself to others—and not just his money. He blessed many people with the peace and joy he received from his Lord by resting in His redemption.

In the wonderful book *Abandonment to Divine Providence,* revered eighteenth-century cleric Jean Pierre De-Caussade describes this wonderful rest we can have when we abandon ourselves to God:

> Every moment of our lives can be a kind of communion with [God's] love.... The most holy of lives is a mysterious thing because of its very simplicity and apparently humble state.... Our master is the Holy Spirit, who gives us these words of life, and all we say to others must come from him.[2]

WHAT IS REST?

Too often, well-meaning and sincere Christians have missed this central message of redemption: the true rest of the believer. The Westminster Catechism teaches, "Man's chief end is to glorify God, and to enjoy him forever."[3]

Relationship with God is to be filled with delight, enjoyment, and the mystery of divine romance. Enjoying God means living our lives filled with His peace and love, free from fear, doubt, worry, anger, and other negative mind-sets. In short, it means resting in Him. The Scriptures teach that

SINCERE CHRISTIANS HAVE MISSED THIS CENTRAL MESSAGE OF REDEMPTION: THE TRUE REST OF THE BELIEVER.

when we truly place our faith in Christ, we can enter into His divine rest: "For we which have believed do enter into rest" (Heb. 4:3).

In contrast, man-centered religion demands self-effort that "rests" in its own self-righteous works. Even good things like giving and prayer are reduced to religious self-effort if we do not learn to enter into rest in Christ's redemption. Too often, the church has opted for this self-effort throughout history. Miguel de Molinos, a devout Spanish priest of the seventeenth century, wrote a book called *The Spiritual Guide* in 1675, in which he explained the two kinds of religious life, *external* and *internal:*

> Those who follow [the external religious life] seek God through their reason and imagination and by means of abstinence and mortification of the senses. They try to visualize God—as a pastor, a physician, a father or a lord. They delight in continually speaking of God, very often making fervent acts of love. By this method they desire to be great.... [It] is the way of beginners...yet by it there is no arriving at perfection, as experience shows in the case of many who, after fifty years of this external exercise, are void of God and full of themselves.
>
> But there are others who live an internal life... resigning themselves wholly into the hands of God and

going with an uplifted spirit into the presence of the Lord, by the means of pure faith…with great assurance, founded in tranquility and inner rest.[4]

For his teaching, which embodied this central message of resting in God's redemption, Molinos was ostracized by the Catholic Church and put into a cell for life, so vehemently attached was the church to the "external" religious life. Yet it is this interior life of communion with God that leads us into His divine rest for which Christ ultimately died; it is divine redemption.

Oswald Chambers writes in his book *If You Will Ask* that the basis of all prayer is not human earnestness, not human need, not the human will; it is *redemption*, and its living center is a personal Holy Spirit. Intimate relationship with God Himself is the goal of the Holy Spirit's work in the life of every believer.[5]

Communion with God is only possible as we learn to yield to the Holy Spirit and seek Him to guide us into all truth (John 16:13). He will show us "the path of life" (Ps. 16:11) and lead us into the restful peace and joy that Christ offers to those who choose to abide in Him. More than just physical rest, the heart of every person yearns for this spiritual communion with God.

Yet how many Christians truly believe that redemption through faith in Christ offers them the enjoyment of indescribable peace, joy, and divine rest? Are you living a life of delightful, intimate relationship with your Lord, basking in the pool of His grace as displayed in the life of my friend? Are you abandoned to resting in the river of His love? Is the Holy Spirit filling you with divine love for God and for others?

Or do you just talk religion, recite platitudes, and follow tradition with an intellectual assent to biblical principles? Are you trying to find redemption on the merit of your own works? Is yours merely an external religion? That path will lead to the weariness, unhappiness, worry, and negative attitudes my friend's wife displayed throughout her life. It robbed her of the enjoyment of communion with God as well as the genuine love her husband longed to share in their marriage. The fact is, it is possible to think you are living the Christian life and never truly enjoy the rest of His redemption.

Understanding r-e-s-t

R-e-s-t. Just seeing the word itself may help you locate your life struggles that rob you of that desirable state of spirit, mind, and body. It may bring to mind your favorite way to relax, kick back, and recreate. Hopefully, contemplating this wonderful reality of rest stirs in your heart a longing to experience the peace, serenity, and sense of well-being that God's divine rest offers you.

Usually when we speak of rest, we are referring to resting our bodies and our minds from the rigors of everyday living, working, and other responsibilities. That is the primary meaning of *rest*, according to Webster's dictionary: "repose, sleep; specifically: a bodily state characterized by minimal functional and metabolic activities."[6]

While physical rest is vital to our well-being, that is not the rest we crave most as human beings. Physical cessation from activity alone will not bring the rest to our hearts and minds that we were created to enjoy. A more profound definition of rest is "peace of mind or spirit."[7] It is this sublime *spiritual* rest that we yearn for most. Without experiencing

true spiritual rest, we cannot find true happiness or fulfillment in life, no matter how hard or where we search for it.
Even our physical rest is compromised without experiencing
true spiritual rest.

THE "DOOR" TO SPIRITUAL REST

This spiritual rest is a result of coming to Christ with faith, a
deep spiritual conviction, and entering into personal relationship with Him. Receiving His forgiveness for our sin
restores our relationship to God, which
Adam and Eve lost through their disobedience. Jesus taught that we must
be "born again" (John 3:7) to receive
the gift of eternal life that He pur-
chased for our redemption through
His death on the cross. Confessing our
sinful state and asking for cleansing
through His precious blood grants us
entrance into our personal peace with
God: "Therefore being justified by

**MORE THAN
JUST PHYSICAL
REST, THE
HEART OF
EVERY PERSON
YEARNS FOR
SPIRITUAL
COMMUNION
WITH GOD.**

faith, we have peace with God through our Lord Jesus Christ"
(Rom. 5:1).

Yet that is just the beginning of our restoration to spiritual rest. In any human friendship, it is as we spend time
with each other, share hearts, and build trust that we forge
enduring relationships. So with Christ, we must abandon
our hearts to Him and continually seek the Holy Spirit to
reveal His love, His will, and His purpose to us. Spending
time with Him by reading His Word, praying, and waiting
on Him forges the strength of relationship that ultimately
restores us to divine rest in every area of our lives. As we

cultivate that intimate relationship with Christ, we learn to enjoy God and glorify Him in all we do.

Recently I received a note from my friend and author Dr. Richard Swenson, which he signed: "In His will is our peace." Of course, he was quoting Dante Alighieri, considered one of the greatest poets in all literature (1265–1321). Author of the *Divine Comedy*, Dante painted a forceful picture of hell as well as paradise. His writings portrayed the truth that apart from our Creator-Redeemer we cannot know peace and rest. It is in doing His will that we will know the satisfying relationship our hearts crave and that brings us peace. It is as the poet wrote: "In His will is our peace."[8]

MISSING THE MARK

Hamartia, the Greek word that means "to miss the mark or to err,"[9] describes our lives when we are absorbed totally in the activities of the world. Our lives are filled with distractions that keep us from knowing God and resting in His redemption.

Personal relationship with God can be hindered by the seemingly innocent *hamartias* of life. They may occur in many ways, but especially by placing our worship in places such as TV, sports, the stock market, beautiful women or men, social status, or anything temporal that we value more than our worship of God. If we spend more time and sense more fervor for this world's interests, we need to refocus our affections and priorities on God to cultivate relationship with Him. Anything less is missing the mark.

IN HIS WILL
IS OUR PEACE.
—DANTE

Consider where the bulk of your recreational or free time

is spent. If you feel you are too busy to spend time with God in prayer, reading His Word, or helping the needy, you may be caught in *hamartia*.

You may be legitimately involved in many things in this world, but they need to be measured against the strength of your pursuit of God. Don't waste your life by missing the mark and failing to pursue the true satisfaction found only in resting in His redemption.

There is a process of learning to abide continually in Christ. It is characterized by a growing desire for divine relationship, communion, and fellowship with your Creator-Redeemer. The peace and joy and rest we experience in this love relationship with God ultimately lead us into our personal destiny, which He has ordained for us. And it makes us effective in all we do in life.

When we do not cultivate this divine intimacy with our Lord, no matter how well intentioned our lives, they will simply fall apart. Only as we learn to rest in God's redemption do we find the spiritual satisfaction for which our hearts are longing.

Unrest caused by fear

In their book *Sleeping With Bread: Holding What Gives You Life*, Dennis, Sheila, and Matthew Linn tell the famous story of orphans after World War II who were alone in Europe and left to starve. The Allied soldiers began gathering them up and placing them in refugee camps, where they were rescued from their plight of imminent starvation. Though they were well-fed and cared for, the children became restless at night and could not sleep. For years, they had experienced so much trauma, hunger, and misery that they simply could not imagine that tomorrow would bring them more food and safety. Their unconscious fear of hunger made them restless.

Someone had the idea to wrap a slice of bread for each child to hold in their hand after they were put to bed. They were not to eat it, just to hold it. When the orphans held in their hands the promise of food for tomorrow, they began to sleep peacefully through the night. Their fear of hunger was appeased in that simple act of love.[10]

RELATIONSHIP WITH GOD CAN BE HINDERED BY THE SEEMINGLY INNOCENT *HAMARTIAS* OF LIFE.

In a similar way, how often do our fears keep us from resting in the goodness of God and receiving His provision for our lives? We too need to hold in our hands the promise of the "bread of life" for tomorrow. The apostle Paul instructed the young minister, Timothy: "For God hath not given us the spirit of fear; but of power, and of love, and of a sound mind" (2 Tim. 1:7). Embracing this wonderful truth and other similar promises will eliminate restlessness from our souls.

Our relationship with God should be reflective of the apostle Paul's words: living in power, in love, and with a sound mind. The power of God will give us courage to confront life's challenges in love. It will empower us to fulfill God's purpose for our lives. And it will destroy the power of fear that keeps us from enjoying life.

The love of God, for which we were created, casts out all the torments of fear (1 John 4:18). As we pursue this love relationship with our Redeemer, He fills us with Himself—all the attributes of His divine love. Our peace and contentment are a result of knowing that God cares for us and will protect us in every circumstance. In that blessed state of mind, we are free to love God and others, to face life courageously, and to enjoy His gift of a sound mind with freedom from the torment of fear. Resting in His redemption lets us experience life that overflows into works that glorify God:

> Herein is my Father glorified, that ye bear much fruit; so shall ye be my disciples.... Ye have not chosen me, but I have chosen you, and ordained you, that ye should go and bring forth fruit, and that your fruit should remain: that whatsoever ye shall ask of the Father in my name, he may give it you.
>
> —JOHN 15:8, 16

Fear results from not knowing God or trusting Him enough to abandon our lives to Him. It is the love of God that we desperately need to set us free from fear. Then our lives will become meaningful and we will know true rest and satisfaction.

MANKIND'S CHIEF END

St. Augustine, the renowned early church father, opened his famous theological treatise, *Confessions,* describing the chief end of mankind, the ultimate purpose for creation:

> Thou hast formed us for Thyself, and our hearts are restless till they find rest in Thee.... Oh! how shall I find rest in Thee? Who will send Thee into my heart to inebriate it, that I may forget my woes, and embrace Thee my only good?... Alas! alas! tell me of Thy compassion, O Lord my God, what Thou art to me. Say

unto my soul, "I am thy salvation. So speak that I may hear. Behold, Lord, the ears of my heart are before Thee; open Thou them, and say unto my soul, "I am thy salvation." When I hear, may I run and lay hold on Thee. Hide not Thy face from me. Let me die, lest I die, if only I may see Thy face.[11]

Our Creator-Redeemer formed us to live in perpetual communion with Him. Have you considered this most profound aspect of your creature-needs for true *spiritual* rest?

> **FOR GOD HATH NOT GIVEN US THE SPIRIT OF FEAR; BUT OF POWER, AND OF LOVE, AND OF A SOUND MIND.**
>
> —2 TIMOTHY 1:7

For peace of mind? For the divine communion with God that St. Augustine cried out for? Have you considered that God alone is your source for ultimate enjoyment, contentment, and fulfillment of your destiny in life?

Or are you one of many who are busy just trying to find a way to enjoy a little physical rest and recreation? A little psychological relief in your favorite escape? Just plodding through each day, trying to be in control of your life, hoping for a little less grief tomorrow? Relief is ill hoped-for unless you pursue the purpose for which you were created: "to glorify God and enjoy Him forever."

I believe it is the longing for this true spiritual rest, so desperately needed and so little understood, that drives millions of people to the pharmacy in search of drugs they hope will artificially induce the relief they seek. Others may try to escape their restlessness and lack of peace through the use of illicit drugs, alcohol, or other equally harmful and inadequate means to find the rest only their Creator can give.

SPIRITUAL SENSITIVITY

Spiritual sensitivity is a phrase that many people use to describe any attempt to find a deeper meaning in life than the physical or material world offers. In that sense, people who pursue spiritual reality in religions other than Christianity use the phrase "spiritual sensitivity" as well. They are aware that there is another dimension to life greater than what they see or feel with the senses. That is a fact. But it is dangerous to pursue the spiritual world apart from faith in Christ.

To develop a godly sense of spiritual sensitivity, we must submit to the biblical truths regarding the one true God, our Father—who is Spirit. Jesus said, "I am the way, the truth, and the life: no man cometh unto the Father, but by me" (John 14:6). And He said that God is a Spirit and that they who worship Him must worship Him in spirit and in truth (John 4:24). When we receive Christ as Savior, Jesus said we are born again of the Spirit (John 3:3, 5). From that moment on, we must learn to cultivate our spiritual sensitivity to God, our heavenly Father.

The apostle Paul said he was a minister of this "mystery which hath been hid from ages and from generations" (Col. 1:26). He said that God wants to make known to believers the "riches of the glory of this mystery among the Gentiles; which is Christ in you, the hope of glory" (v. 27). Paul also taught that the Spirit of the Lord brings liberty to our hearts and that as we continually behold Him, we "are changed into the same image from glory to glory, even as by the Spirit of the Lord" (2 Cor. 3:17–18).

True spiritual sensitivity is a result of becoming alive to God in your spirit and learning to live in communion with Him. That intimate relationship with God will be reflected in your living a godly life; that spiritual sensitivity involves learning who the Creator is, what He has done to make life beautiful, and discovering the true meaning and purpose for life.

OUR CREATOR-REDEEMER FORMED US TO LIVE IN PERPETUAL COMMUNION WITH HIM.

Some are inspired to cultivate relationship with their Creator when they observe, as I did, the brilliant construction of a single cell as viewed under the microscope—the sub-cellular molecules that are the basic building blocks of all of life. Others see God's handiwork in nature, viewing awesome mountain peaks, ocean waves, or a beautiful sunset, and are humbled to seek the God who created such majesty.

Still others discover spiritual reality by observing caring people who selflessly give their energies and time to those who are hurting in their bodies or minds. There are other people who cultivate spiritual sensitivity in response to their own godly enthusiasm as a result of knowing that God loves them and wants to engage in relationship with them.

In whatever way you discover the spiritual dimension of life in Christ for which you were created, the entire process has been initiated by the divine work of God within you. He made you in His image, which is Spirit. And He wants to redeem you back to Himself, to commune with Him in spirit and truth (John 4:24).

Do you have time for the divine? Do you seek God to give you a greater spiritual sensitivity in relationship with Him? That is what His heart of love desires. Every human heart beats with a deep longing for this mystery of a divine romance with their Creator, and that desire was placed there by God and cannot be fulfilled by a lesser suitor. Yet how many never realize with St. Augustine that we were made for God and that "our hearts are restless till they find rest in Thee"?[12]

Recently, as I was listening to Fernando Ortega sing the wonderful hymn "My Redeemer," I felt the awe of that spiritual dimension fill my heart. As I listened to the words, I basked in the awesome privilege of finding my personal rest in His redemption. I have included the lyrics here for you to ponder the wonder of God's redemption, His love for you:

> I will sing of my Redeemer
> And His wondrous love to me;
> On the cruel cross He suffered,
> From the curse to set me free.
>
> Sing, oh sing, of my Redeemer,
> With His blood, He purchased me,
> On the cross, He sealed my pardon,
> Paid the debt, and made me free.
>
> I will tell the wondrous story
> How my lost estate to save,
> In His boundless love and mercy,
> He the ransom freely gave.
>
> I will praise my dear Redeemer,
> His triumphant power I'll tell,
> How the victory He giveth
> Over sin, and death, and hell.
>
> I will sing of my Redeemer,
> And His heav'nly love to me;
> He from death to life hath brought me,
> Son of God with Him to be.[13]

GOD'S HEART FOR MANKIND

God created mankind on the sixth day of His creative work, during which He called into being the universe and all of creation as we know it. That was the last day of God's work of creation. What we learn next from the Scriptures may seem a little strange: after six days of creative work, God rested:

> And on the seventh day God ended his work which he had made; and he rested on the seventh day from all his work which he had made.
> —GENESIS 2:2

One can hardly deduce from that statement that God was tired. An omnipotent God would not have needed to recuperate from His magnificent work of creation, would He? Yet God reserved a day of rest, a time for ceasing from all activity, to celebrate the work He had done. He blessed that seventh day because He rested from all His work (v. 3).

Later, God called that day of rest the Sabbath (Hebrew: *shabbath*), which means "to repose, desist from exertion, celebrate."[14] Have you considered what significance there might be in the fact that mankind's first full day of life was the day of God's *shabbath*? Rest. Celebration. What a lovely way for mankind, God's jewel of creation, to begin life!

It is as we are restored through redemption to the purity of that environment of spiritual rest that we will fulfill the true works for which He created us. Rather than our self-righteous efforts to make a name for ourselves, we will discover the true meaning of life: "For we are his workmanship, created in Christ Jesus unto good works, which God hath before ordained that we should walk in them" (Eph. 2:10). Otherwise, all our self-effort will result only in weariness or a sense of pride, not in the peace and joy that come from fulfilling God's will for our lives.

The Book of Genesis tells us that God created mankind in His image (Gen. 1:27). And, as I mentioned, the Scriptures teach us that God is Spirit (John 4:24). That spiritual image of God within us continually desires to experience *shabbath*: the rest of God. When God made a requirement for mankind to keep a *shabbath* as a day of rest from all labor (Exod. 20:10–11), it was to give man a temporal, physical rest that reflects the spiritual rest for which we long.

SPIRITUAL SENSITIVITY INVOLVES LEARNING WHO THE CREATOR IS.

Of course, it is the spiritual rest of living in continual harmony with the Creator for which our souls yearn most. We were created for God. Without His continual presence in our lives, we are doomed to unrest and unhappiness.

God is not only Spirit; God is love (1 John 4:8). The entire message of the Bible reveals that the purpose of God in creating mankind was to have a family—sons and daughters with whom He could have fellowship and share His love. The great, loving heart of God designed mankind to know happiness and fulfillment only through an intimate relationship with Him. He wants us to celebrate life with Him as He ordained it to be.

According to God's original plan, the mystery and romance of divine love were to be consummated in each human heart as each one chose to live life in the presence of God. That they would rest in absolute safety and bliss in their Creator, receiving the love of God and accepting all of His gifts with joy—that was the heart of God for mankind.

From the beginning of creation, the concept of resting in God's love is the basic model of how we are to live life. That is how we were created to enjoy the fulfillment that our hearts crave. There, in that continual communion with God, we learn how to fulfill the works He has ordained for us. The psalmist understood this truth:

> Thou wilt shew me the path of life: in thy presence is fulness of joy; at thy right hand there are pleasures for evermore.
>
> —Psalm 16:11

God's Plan for Redemption

That first couple blew it. They contaminated the entire human race when they decided to live independently from God and be in charge of their own lives. God turned man over to the consequences of his sin. Physical death entered the scene, spiritual death became a reality, and there was no hope of redemption to be found in man's own efforts. The only hope was the promise of the coming of the Redeemer—the Son of God—and in the promised enablement of the Holy Spirit for all who seek Him:

> And ye shall seek me, and find me, when ye shall search for me with all your heart. And I will be found of you, saith the Lord.
>
> —Jeremiah 29:13–14

God calls mankind to choose to live in His love and to seek relationship with Him. That is the true nature of love: it is a relationship based on fulfilled desire, not on keeping rules. The mystery of love involves a mutual reciprocation of two hearts that cherish each other and want to live in harmony together. Out of that love, they are willing to accept any conditions placed on the relationship to avoid disrupting the harmony they enjoy.

When Adam and Eve chose to disobey God, they disrupted the harmony of that divine romance. As a result, they lost the source of the divine rest they craved, which was to be found only in satisfying fellowship with their Creator. When that happened, God began the long, arduous task of redeeming mankind, calling us back to the blissful rest for which we were created. Down through the centuries of mankind's existence, God continually reached down to us, working His plan of redemption.

> **WHEN SIN ENTERED THE PICTURE, GOD REVEALED HIS PLAN OF REDEMPTION TO BRING US BACK INTO RELATIONSHIP WITH HIM.**

Redemption defined

Before we can truly appreciate the wonder of resting in His redemption, we need to understand the significance of the word. *Redemption* means "the act of delivering from sin or saving from evil." It also signifies the "purchasing back of something previously sold."[15] When Adam and Eve "sold out" to the devil's lie that by disobeying God they would become as gods, it became necessary for God to purchase back lost mankind from the clutches of evil. He would have to redeem mankind so they could once again become sons and daughters who would walk in fellowship with Him.

Divine Rest in the Old Testament

The essence of the entire message of over thirty thousand verses in the Bible is this reality of enjoying an intimate relationship with God. It is this central truth of the Scriptures that leads our sin-sick souls back to the rest for which we were created. That was God's desire even for Old Testament saints who lived before the victory of Calvary.

The fall of mankind into sin through Adam and Eve's disobedience did not catch God by surprise. God planned the redemption of mankind before the creation of the world. The Scriptures refer to Christ as "the Lamb slain from the foundation of the world" (Rev. 13:8). The essence of the Old Testament is the story of God enacting this divine plan of redemption through His prophets, priests, and kings who helped to guide His people back to His rest.

THE ESSENCE OF THE ENTIRE BIBLE IS THE DIVINE LOVE STORY OF GOD REACHING DOWN TO MAN TO REDEEM HIM BACK TO HIMSELF.

For example, when God called Israel to be a nation, He redeemed them through the hand of Moses from their cruel bondage to Pharaoh. You remember the provision He made to spare the firstborn of Israel by having them place the blood of a lamb on the doorposts of their homes. As they did so in obedience to His Word, they were saying, in effect, "We rest in God's redemption." They trusted His word to them that He would protect them from the scourge of death that was coming to judge the Egyptians.

And He did "pass over" those homes where the blood of

the lamb was applied. God instituted the feast of Passover to celebrate that deliverance from destruction. As they celebrated this Passover feast, they were acknowledging God's power to bring them as a nation to the doorway of faith.

When God gave Moses detailed instructions in the wilderness to build a tabernacle, He was once again seeking a way to dwell with His people, to be near them, and to give them His rest. God longed to commune with them, so He told Moses to make a mercy seat, a golden lid over the ark of the covenant, where the blood of the atonement would be sprinkled. And God said He would meet with His high priest there. It would be the dwelling place of God's glory where He could speak to mankind again. There He would show them mercy and let them experience relationship with Him. He would speak to them there, guiding and directing them and giving them power over their enemies.

After the tabernacle was built, the Israelites marched toward Canaan, the Promised Land, where God had said they would live. He promised to be with them to conquer the enemies that dwelled in the land. However, when they arrived, they realized there were giants in the land. And the cities there had high thick walls, which the people were afraid they could not conquer.

Joshua and Caleb reminded the people that God was with them and would help them conquer the land He had promised to give to them. But the people refused to trust God's word. Because they would not believe the word of God to them, they were forced to wander in the wilderness for the rest of their lives. Everyone of that generation who gave in to fear instead of grabbing the promise in faith died in that wilderness wandering. Only then did the second generation get to march into the Promised Land.

The only exceptions to this sad fate were Joshua and Caleb, men from the first generation who had believed the Lord's promise and declared it to the people. Joshua led Israel into the Promised Land. He prepared them for battle, and they began to conquer the enemies in the land. Caleb asked for a mountain in the Promised Land and was granted the strength to conquer it. They were victorious because they chose to trust in the promises of God and to rest in His provision.

Though the Israelites had come out of Egypt (which is a type of "sin"), their redemption from that captivity did not automatically teach them to rest in God's love, His power, and His redemption. Because they refused to trust God to give them all He had promised, He would not let them enter the Promised Land of His rest. The New Testament teaches that it was their unbelief, their lack of faith, that kept them from receiving the rest He had promised them.

THE CALL TO SPIRITUAL REST

God repeatedly called men and women in the Old Testament to enter into His rest. He wanted them to experience the intimate relationship with their Creator-Redeemer that He had ordained from the beginning. King David, also known as the sweet psalmist of Israel, understood that God's redemptive rest was a reality for those who would seek Him through prayer and meditation on His Word:

> Commit thy way unto the LORD; trust also in him; and he shall bring it to pass.... Rest in the LORD, and wait patiently for him.
>
> —PSALM 37:5, 7

The Book of Psalms also declares, "For the LORD hath chosen Zion; he hath desired it for his habitation. This is my rest for ever: here will I dwell; for I have desired it" (Ps. 132:13–14). Again, God revealed His choosing to dwell with mankind and let them enjoy the spiritual rest of His presence.

OLD TESTAMENT SAINTS UNDERSTOOD THE REST THAT WAS AVAILABLE TO THEM FROM GOD.

He delights to be our God, our heavenly Father. And He longs to dwell among us. If God is content to dwell with us and let us hear His voice, then it is foolish for us not to be content to rest in His love, to commune with Him through personal prayer and worship.

When Jesus came to the earth to become our Redeemer, He confirmed the Father's desire for intimate fellowship with us:

> If a man love me, he will keep my words: and my Father will love him, and we will come unto him, and make our abode with him.
>
> —JOHN 14:23

Since the moment sin entered the world through Adam and Eve's disobedience, God has been working His plan to redeem, to buy back, all that He lost as a consequence. He is determined to enjoy the mystery of the divine romance for which He created mankind originally.

The saints in the Old Testament had trials in their lives that distracted them and kept them from entering the rest of God. The psalmist knew that there was only one thing to do when that happened: "Return unto thy rest, O my soul; for the LORD hath dealt bountifully with thee" (Ps. 116:7).

Likewise, when we get distracted from focusing on living in God's presence, we need to recognize the reason we say "I am uneasy," "I am restless," "I am trusting in my own efforts," or "I am worrying and full of fear." And we need to say to ourselves, as the psalmist did, "I must go back to the wonderful place of rest in God's love and redemption. There my heart will be at peace and God's Spirit will comfort me and strengthen me and give me all I need to confront life's situations."

> **PRAYER IS MEANT TO BE OUR HEART'S EXPRESSION OF DIVINE COMMUNION WITH OUR REDEEMER.**

Many years after the kingdom of Israel became a divided kingdom, God was still reaching out to His wayward people. Through the prophet Isaiah, He declared His remedy for our plight:

> All we like sheep have gone astray; we have turned every one to his own way; and the LORD hath laid on him the iniquity of us all.
>
> —ISAIAH 53:6

Here Isaiah describes, prophetically, our Savior, Jesus Christ, on whom our iniquity would ultimately be laid. He also says, "He was wounded for our transgressions, he was bruised for our iniquities: the chastisement of our peace was upon him; and with his stripes we are healed" (Isa. 53:5). Isaiah looked forward hundreds of years to the fulfillment of God's ultimate plan for redemption, seeing that it would require the laying of the sin of the whole world upon God's only Son, Jesus, the spotless Lamb of God.

In the "type" of the Passover and the mercy seat of the ark, God had already introduced a picture of the ultimate blood sacrifice of our Lord Jesus Christ. He spoke again through His prophet Isaiah, revealing His plan for Christ's coming:

> And in that day there shall be a root of Jesse, which shall stand for an ensign of the people; to it shall the Gentiles seek: and his rest shall be glorious.
>
> —ISAIAH 11:10

This glorious rest is only possible as God's truth overcomes our error and sin and His light overcomes our spiritual darkness. Jesus came into the world to live as the Light of the world (John 8:12). He also revealed Himself as the way, the truth, and the life (John 14:6) who had come to redeem us from spiritual darkness and deliver us from the lies of the evil one.

Isaiah, who prophesied during the reign of King Hezekiah, declared this promise of God's rest for the people: "For thus saith the Lord GOD, the Holy One of Israel; in returning and rest shall ye be saved; in quietness and in confidence shall be your strength" (Isa. 30:15).

Much later, just before Jerusalem was destroyed by the enemies of Israel, God raised up the prophet Jeremiah to call the people back to His rest:

> Thus saith the LORD, Stand ye in the ways, and see, and ask for the old paths, where is the good way, and walk therein, and ye shall find rest for your souls.
>
> —JEREMIAH 6:16

Even though they said, "We will not walk therein" (Jer. 6:16), their constant refusal to return to God's rest did not deter His loving heart from pursuing them. The entire Old

Testament is filled with God's voice summoning His people to respond to His call of love, to return to His paths where they would find His rest. Many times they refused to hear the heart of God. Yet He continued to reveal His desire to redeem them to relationship with Him.

CHRIST WOULD PERSONALLY ATONE FOR EVERY PERSON'S SIN AGAINST GOD.

Through the centuries, God prepared His people to receive His Son, Jesus, who would offer the ultimate atonement for sin, giving His lifeblood for the salvation of the whole world. Christ would personally atone for every person's sin against God. He would redeem us back to our rightful place of resting in His redemption. It is up to each one of us to receive the wonderful redemption love that God offers to us.

PERSONAL MEDITATION

CHAPTER 1

Is prayer essential to our communion with God?

_____

_____

Oswald Chambers says that the purpose of all prayer is that we may know God. Do you agree?

_____

_____

As a Christian, can you experience divine peace and a sense of well-being without resting in His redemption?

_____

_____

According to St. Augustine, our hearts are restless until they find their rest in God. Do you agree?

_____

_____

Is Christ the only way to eternal life? (See John 14:6.)

_____

_____

A sinner can no more repent and believe without the Holy Spirit's aid than he can create a world.

—CHARLES SPURGEON[1]

The whole purpose of the redemption is to give back to man the original source of life, and in a regenerated man this means "Christ formed in you."

—OSWALD CHAMBERS[2]

2

RECEIVING GOD'S REDEMPTION

RECENTLY, I PLAYED golf with a fellow ophthalmologist from Michigan. In conversation, I soon learned that he attends a Greek Orthodox Church. When he asked me what church I attend, I told him I attended different churches. Then we began discussing the fact that the church you attend is not the most important aspect of your relationship with God. Rather, the key to enjoying relationship with God is your personal response to His redemption. Also, it is who you are inside that counts.

Redemption has little to do with the governmental structure of your denomination, its regulations, or even its doctrinal positions. Redemption is all about Jesus, His sacrifice for sin at Calvary, and our response to that redemptive act for us personally. From that perspective, we understand that resting in God's redemption is a common theme for all of the streams of the Judeo-Christian faith.

However, without personally accepting the forgiveness of God through faith in Christ, you can become a renowned church leader and still know nothing about resting in His redemption. It is only through regeneration by the power of the Holy Spirit in our spirit that we are made alive to God, who is Spirit.

Jesus said, "I tell you the truth, unless you are born again, you cannot see the Kingdom of God.... I assure you, no one can enter the Kingdom of God without being born of water and the Spirit. Humans can reproduce only human life, but the Holy Spirit gives birth to spiritual life" (John 3:3, 5–6, NLT).

As my friend and I discussed these basic spiritual concepts, he recognized that as long as we focus on being followers of Christ, we can fellowship together as believers, no matter how different our church polity might be. Receiving God's redemption through faith in Christ is the prerequisite for being restored to divine rest in His love. That is the foundation of all Christian life.

DOES JESUS LIVE IN YOUR HOUSE?

When I speak to groups of people, I often ask them, "Does Jesus live in your house?" Many times their first response is, "We go to church." Then I repeat, "But does Jesus live in your house, and do you live in His love?" Often they respond, "We love God."

That is good, but that was not my question. Learning to live in the love of Christ is very different from expressing our love for Him. For years, I attended church and told God that I loved Him. I was trying to love Him and, as a scientist, to show Him my respect for the ingenuity of divine design I saw in all of creation. I thanked Him for His divine incarnation and for bringing salvation to the world.

But in the living of my life, I realized how little love I had for others. I began to understand that love was not natural to fallen humanity. I began to see my need to, first of all, learn to *rest in His love* by receiving His grace, mercy, and redemption. Intellectual response to God's goodness is not the same as receiving Him into my heart and abandoning myself to continually receive His awesome love.

The idea of loving God is appealing and very important; however, it cannot be compared to the importance of focusing on the omnipotence of God's love for us. When we receive the love of God, we recognize that He is love. Then we realize how much our love is lacking. We learn that God's love is supreme, that He is all-powerful, and that He is the first cause of the existence of all things (Col. 1:16–17). That

> LEARNING TO LIVE IN THE LOVE OF CHRIST IS VERY DIFFERENT FROM EXPRESSING OUR LOVE FOR HIM.

divine love, God Himself, is the eternal power that transcends time and allows those who love Him to dwell with Him throughout eternity.

When I began to focus on God's love for me, in that intimate place of divine communion with the Lord, I began to see His love manifest in my life to others. And I knew that I was discovering the mystery of divine romance that would result in my learning to rest in His redemption. I would not be limited by my small human love; the love of God would be reflected in my life so that I could love others and glorify Him in all I do.

ACCEPTING THE ATONEMENT

The Bible says that we love God because He first loved us (1 John 4:19). It is in receiving His love for us that we will continually fall in love with Him, becoming more and more enthralled with our Creator-Redeemer. Anything less than this intimate love relationship results in a "works religion," characterized by drudgery, duty, and defeat.

As I have mentioned, before we can learn to rest in God's redemption, we must first *receive* it. We must accept by faith Christ's atonement for our sin through His death on Calvary. Faith is not mental assent to Bible doctrine; it is a deep spiritual conviction that grips the heart and brings supernatural transformation of our desires, goals, and pursuits in life.

BEFORE WE CAN LEARN TO REST IN GOD'S REDEMPTION, WE MUST FIRST *RECEIVE* IT WITH FAITH—DEEP SPIRITUAL CONVICTION.

When Jesus said that you must be born again to see the kingdom of God, He was speaking of a real transaction between your spirit and the Holy Spirit. That experience is what makes you alive to God, restores your spiritual communion with Him, and allows you to receive His love and His atonement for your sin. Until that happens, according to the Scriptures, we are "dead in trespasses and sins" (Eph. 2:1).

The biblical word *atonement* signifies "another has taken my place, has suffered the death I deserve because of my sin" (Strong's Hebrew: 3722). Simply stated, *atonement* means that the judgment I deserve has been executed upon another so that I may go free. To receive this grace of redemption for my sins, the Bible says to call upon the name of the Lord: "For whosoever shall call upon the name of the Lord shall be saved" (Rom. 10:13).

In the moment we call on the name of the Lord, the Holy

Spirit gives us faith to believe the promise of God for salvation through the Lamb of God alone, "which taketh away the sin of the world" (John 1:29).

When we receive Christ's forgiveness for our sin, God gives to us His peace and righteousness through the death and resurrection of Christ, who has taken our place in judgment. The apostle Paul declared:

> Therefore being justified by faith, we have peace with God through our Lord Jesus Christ.
>
> —ROMANS 5:1

RIGHTEOUSNESS THROUGH FAITH

Through God's plan of redemption, the apostle Paul explained that righteousness is imputed to us through our faith in Christ (Rom. 4:21–24). *Imputation* is a bookkeeping term that describes putting something of value into someone's account. Legally, before God's judgment bar, when you believe in the atonement of the Lord Jesus, accepting Him as your Redeemer, the righteousness of Christ is imputed to your account as your legal right to stand before God.

When God looks at you as a believer in Christ, He considers you to be righteous because of Christ's righteousness. He bought your righteousness through Christ's sacrifice on Calvary. Your redemption is given as a gift. It is not based on anything in you or good works that you do. It is based only on what Jesus did in atoning for your sin on the cross and your receiving His saving grace through faith in Him.

No salvation through our "self-righteous works"

There is no other way to experience restored communion with God. No matter how well-intentioned we may be, we have no merit in ourselves, for according to the Scriptures, "all have sinned, and come short of the glory of God" (Rom. 3:23). After Adam and Eve sinned, all of humanity was infected with that sin nature, that selfish, disobedient bent to live independently and rule our own lives. But when we accept Christ by faith as our Savior from sin, God forgives us of all our sin and gives us the righteousness that is from Christ Himself:

> But it is from Him that you have your life in Christ Jesus, Whom God made our Wisdom from God…our Righteousness…and our Consecration…and our Redemption [providing our ransom from eternal penalty for sin].
> —1 CORINTHIANS 1:30, AMP

Only when we understand that we cannot make ourselves righteous will we cease from our own self-righteous works.

THE HOLY SPIRIT GIVES US FAITH TO BELIEVE THE PROMISE OF GOD FOR SALVATION THROUGH THE LAMB OF GOD.

Until then, resting in His redemption is not possible. We must believe that God gives us His righteousness through faith in Christ alone. As we truly believe in Christ through the working of the Holy Spirit in our lives, we are filled with sheer gratitude and humility. We bow our hearts to worship Him for His wonderful redemption of our souls and for the peace we have received that we could find in no other pursuit.

In receiving that divine wisdom, we begin a journey that will lead us more deeply into intimate fellowship with Christ, our Redeemer. It is at this beginning point in our divine romance that we take ourselves off the hook of personal performance, with its nauseating self-righteousness. Instead, we choose to trust in the Lord to be the provider of all we need for life: wisdom, righteousness, consecration (sanctification), and rest in His redemption alone. The apostle Paul described the kingdom of God as "righteousness, and peace, and joy in the Holy Ghost" (Rom. 14:17).

Grace vs. works

Let me mention briefly that, throughout the centuries, there has been an ongoing debate in Christianity regarding the power of *grace* and the place of *works* in a believer's life. Some describe salvation in the way we have, as a result of *imputation* of grace, meaning that God did all we need through Christ to give us the gift of salvation.

Other churches firmly believe in a doctrine of *infusion*, which states that we must first become good enough for the Lord to accept us into His grace. These churches require works, such as monetary giving, service, and other good works, from people to validate their salvation. However, the Scriptures teach clearly that our righteousness is as filthy rags (Isa. 64:6). They assert that salvation is a gift of God and not of works:

> For by grace are ye saved through faith; and that not of yourselves: it is the gift of God: not of works, lest any man should boast.
>
> —EPHESIANS 2:8–9

These and other verses teach that we are saved by faith in Jesus alone. He saved us by His grace, mercy, and love apart from any good work we could do to earn it. Our simple duty is to yield to the work of the Holy Spirit by accepting His salvation and resting in His redemption. In that state of justification and peace with God, we can become purposeful and effective in our lives.

Good works will follow. Out of our love for our Lord and in obedience to His commands, we will learn to glorify Him in all we do. Oswald Chambers concurs:

> Redemption is the reality which alters inability into ability.... The mighty redemption of God is made actual in my experience by the living efficacy of the Holy Ghost.[3]

We must, of course, take responsibility for our actions and for making intelligent decisions regarding our lives *after* receiving Christ's redemption. But we seek His truth first to help us make realistic, honorable, and even scientifically-based decisions. Realism is embodied in truth, who is Christ (John 14:6). We must seek His truth rather than follow our self-righteous desires to earn salvation, which counterfeits truth. It is in our continual, wholehearted pursuit of truth that we will learn to rest in God's redemption.

TRUE SPIRITUAL CONVICTION IS BASED ON TOTAL ABANDONMENT TO GOD'S REDEMPTION.

True spiritual conviction is based on total abandonment to God's redemption. When we receive salvation by faith, we do not doubt God's grace, His power to forgive our sin, or His divine love for us. Simply by believing in God's power to save our souls through the sacrifice of Jesus Christ, the Scriptures teach that we are justified in His sight and receive His peace.

It is this limitless power of the atonement that provides us the grace to have intimate fellowship with Christ. It is through the imputation of His grace to our lives that we can pursue the divine mystery of romance with Him.

In cultivating daily fellowship with God, we will find the fulfillment and satisfaction—the rest—that our souls craves. When the Bible talks of fellowship with God, the Greek word *koinonia* is used. It means "association, communion, joint participation, intercourse, intimacy."[4] We enjoy fellowship with Christ as we continually come to Him to find rest for our souls.

The apostle Paul prayed for the Corinthian church (and, vicariously, for all believers) that "the grace of the Lord Jesus Christ, and the love of God, and the communion [*koinonia*] of the Holy Ghost, be with you all" (2 Cor. 13:14).

As a Christian, have you fully realized the saving power of Christ to reconnect you with God in this intimate way? Do you understand that you are a new creature, born again and alive to God so that you can actually live in communion, fellowship, and intimacy with the Trinity—God the Father, Christ the Son, and the Holy Spirit? Are you enjoying God and glorifying Him in all you do?

As I mentioned in the introduction, the entire motivation of the apostle Paul was to live in communion with Christ, to know Him intimately and bring glory to Him. As you read Paul's stated purpose for living, I invite you to make it your personal prayer:

[For my determined purpose is] that I may know Him [that I may progressively become more deeply and intimately acquainted with Him, perceiving and recognizing and understanding the wonders of His Person more strongly and more clearly], and that I may in that same way come to know the power outflowing from His resurrection [which it exerts over believers], and that I may so share His sufferings as to be continually transformed [in spirit into His likeness even] to His death, [in the hope] that if possible I may attain to the [spiritual and moral] resurrection [that lifts me] out from among the dead [even while in the body]. Not that I have now attained [this ideal], or have already been made perfect, but I press on to lay hold of (grasp) and make my own, that for which Christ Jesus (the Messiah) has laid hold of me and made me His own. I do not consider, brethren, that I have captured and made it my own [yet]; but one thing I do [it is my one aspiration]: forgetting what lies behind and straining forward to what lies ahead, I press on toward the goal to win the [supreme and heavenly] prize to which God in Christ Jesus is calling us upward.

—PHILIPPIANS 3:10–14, AMP

Unless our life's motivation, our "determined purpose," is to live daily in this divine romance, to have ever deepening fellowship and intimacy with Christ, we will never know what it means to rest in His redemption. We may study theology and doctrine, do good works, and exert all our strength to live godly lives, but we will fail miserably. The peace, joy, and rest of God will continually elude us if we depend on our own efforts to please God.

If the essence of Christianity is fellowship with God through His grace, our behavior must reflect the wholehearted pursuit of that divine communion with our Savior. Otherwise, we are doomed to live out the foolishness of our self-righteousness. Our efforts to do good works and behave righteously will undoubtedly fail.

The mystery, joy, and romance of totally abandoning yourself to God's grace and love are the purpose of your atonement through the blood of Christ. This divine purpose is an integral part of the victorious Christian life. You cannot hope to maintain a state of sanity, much less tranquility, without pursuing personal rest in God's redemption. Oswald Chambers describes this divine power found only in God's redemption:

> The effective working of redemption in our experience makes us leap for joy in the midst of things in which other people see nothing but disastrous calamity. When the redemption is effectually at work it always rises to its source, viz., God.[5]

Waiting on God, seeking Him in His Word, and being led by the Holy Spirit are the blessed life of true sons and daughters of God. The apostle Paul wrote, "For as many as are led by the Spirit of God, they are the sons of God" (Rom. 8:14).

YOKED WITH CHRIST

Jesus's invitation to all who will follow Him in truth is to take His yoke, which is easy, and His burden, which is light (Matt. 11:28). Jesus was using a very common agricultural picture to help people understand their relationship with Him. They were very familiar with the scene of an old, experienced ox carrying the brunt of the load and a young ox yoked with him, learning to follow his lead.

As we become yoked together with Christ, we can be sure

that He will bear the heavy burdens of life for us. Our part is to learn to follow His lead in total dependence on Him. Though it may seem difficult at first, our choice to seek Him diligently takes the intolerable burden of ruling our own lives off our shoulders. In that dependent relationship, we receive the rest for our souls for which we yearn. This divine rest is a mystery to many; it is an exhilarating romance to those who truly learn to relax in it.

Resting in His redemption is what true Christianity is all about. It is the reason for the atonement, revealed in type in the Old Testament and fulfilled in reality in the New Testament in Christ. If your life is not characterized by continual abandonment to His grace, you cannot truly call yourself a Christian.

RESTING IN HIS REDEMPTION IS WHAT TRUE CHRISTIANITY IS ALL ABOUT.

In essence, when you work hard to achieve your own righteousness, without fully yielding to the grace of God, you are trying to be your own savior. Those efforts result in self-made religion, which is counterfeit to true Christianity. Christ commanded His followers:

> Abide in me, and I in you. As the branch cannot bear fruit of itself, except it abide in the vine; no more can ye, except ye abide in me. I am the vine, ye are the branches: He that abideth in me, and I in him, the same bringeth forth much fruit: for without me ye can do nothing.
>
> —JOHN 15:4–5

Jesus taught that by abandoning yourself to Christ, you will enjoy the blessed fruits of salvation. Christ is the ultimate fulfillment of the promise of rest given to Old Testament saints. As I mentioned, even those who lived before Christ were promised this life of perfect peace:

> You will guard him and keep him in perfect and constant peace whose mind [both its inclination and its character] is stayed on You, because he commits himself to You, leans on You, and hopes confidently in You.... For thus said the Lord God, the Holy One of Israel: In returning [to Me] and resting [in Me] you shall be saved; in quietness and in [trusting] confidence shall be your strength.
>
> —ISAIAH 26:3; 30:15, AMP

How much more should we, as New Testament believers, enjoy constant peace through Christ, the Prince of Peace? Jesus declared:

> Peace I leave with you, my peace I give unto you: not as the world giveth, give I unto you. Let not your heart be troubled, neither let it be afraid.
>
> —JOHN 14:27

Christian living that is based on an understanding of *resting in His redemption* will fill our lives with days that are like heaven on earth.

Personal Meditation

Chapter 2

How is *redemption* defined? What does it mean for a person to be redeemed?

How does redemption differ from eternal damnation or hell?

Is resting in God's redemption a common theme of Jewish, Catholic, and Protestant belief from both Old and New Testaments?

What part did Christ play in our redemption as a one-time event? As a continuing source of our life of peace?

Does Christ save us by grace through faith alone? Is the work He then gives us to do our opportunity to thank Him for our redemption? (See Ephesians 2:8–10.)

Is true Christianity a divine love story? Is all creation a love story from God?

What is the role of the Holy Spirit in our redemption? In our daily actions?

PART 2

THE BIBLICAL BASIS FOR ALL CHRISTIAN LIVING IS RESTING IN HIS REDEMPTION

It is a great thing to be a believer, but easy to misunderstand what the New Testament means by it. It is not that we believe Jesus Christ can "do" things, or that we believe in a plan of salvation; it is that we believe "him"; whatever happens we will hang in to the fact that he is true.

—OSWALD CHAMBERS[1]

The Lesson of the Widow's Mite
(Mark 12:41–44)
by Pastor Gary Carter

Left alone with none to help
All my thoughts turn in on self
But faith breaks in and sets me free
In the land of the living God's help I'll see.
These copper mites are small and bent
Worth only a fraction of a cent
All I have is in my palm
But "All that is within me" is my psalm
"Bless His holy name and never forget"
"A crown of lovingkindness on my head is set."
When people promise much and let me down
Eternal love resets the crown
Surely there is one worse off than I
God can deliver these, to relieve her sighs.
He is faithful!
I am grateful!
I give it all!
—And Jesus saw!
But why did she not keep the second mite?
Did faith prove to flesh the worth of songs in the
     night?
In the second mite, Jesus saw she gave her heart
And found joy the world cannot give and the world
     cannot part![1]

3

FAITH FOR REDEMPTION

A S AN OPHTHALMOLOGIST, my scientific studies led me into molecular biology. This branch of biology deals with the ultimate physicochemical organization of living matter. It involves the study of some of the tiniest building blocks of life, such as protein molecules, that form the DNA of every form of life.

What scientists are now capable of seeing under the microscope opens an incredible, invisible world where life functions with extravagant precision and design on the molecular level. I have been astounded at the infinite functioning of these tiniest building blocks of life. Their precision of form, their innate healing power, the orderly design of every minute function of the body—all were instrumental in drawing me to belief in a Creator. I became especially enthralled as I studied the eye and observed its astounding capabilities, each of which makes the eye one of the most awesome elements of all creation.

My studies have enabled me to provide healing innovations to my patients. Through the publication of medical textbooks for corneal wound healing and other aspects of refractive cataract surgery, I have been able to help my ophthalmologist colleagues as well. Yet perhaps the most important result of my studies is the spiritual understanding they brought to me. They opened the eyes of my heart to embrace with deep spiritual conviction the wonder of my Creator-Redeemer.

THE MOST IMPORTANT RESULT OF MY STUDIES IS THE SPIRITUAL UNDERSTANDING THEY BROUGHT TO ME.

This extraordinary magnificence of creation that I witnessed under the microscope simply did not fit the theoretical philosophy of evolution I was taught in medical school. In the book I coauthored with my friend Tom Woodward, *Darwinism Under the Microscope,* I explained why I eventually rejected the cultish belief of evolution and the supremacy of science:

> With the encouragement of and under the pedagogy of the scientific community, the primacy of God has been superceded by a belief in the near omnipotence of science and of human knowledge. Stretching our hands toward the "tree of life," seeking, in some manner, not only to displace the Creator but to *become* creator is more than just reckless.... We must realize His redemption, His omniscience, and remain vigilant that we do not lose sight of the greater, deeper truth.
>
> This truth is that life was created by God. We may be its stewards... [but] we can never create life....
>
> The essential attitude toward life should be one of awe, appreciation, and respect while devoid of pride and a desire to transcend or manipulate without discipline.[2]

As my knowledge of the design of human life increased through scientific discovery, it transformed my entire perspective of life. I knew a growing sense of deep appreciation for the astounding gift of life as I observed it under the microscope. That scientific knowledge caused me to begin a pilgrimage toward a deep, intimate relationship with the Designer—the Creator-Redeemer of all of life—that continues until today.

APPRECIATION FOR OUR CREATOR-REDEEMER

In my personal journey to faith in God, the Creator-Redeemer, I have come to believe that a lack of appreciation for our eternal Creator is one of humankind's greatest sins. When these two spiritual realities—appreciation for creation and surrender to our loving Savior—unite in a person's heart, the result is an explosion of hope, love, joy, purpose, and destiny.[3]

Only believers who learn to truly appreciate their Creator can enjoy the eternal benefits of the abundant life Jesus promised: "I am come that they might have life, and that they might have it more abundantly" (John 10:10). That deep appreciation in a believer's heart evokes adoration and worship of God.

Learning to live a life of grateful worship causes us to walk in the power of God's anointing and to fulfill our eternal destiny. That anointed lifestyle, restored to intimate relationship with the Creator-Redeemer, brings the deepest satisfaction available to the human heart. I never tire of reflecting on the wisdom of John Piper's maxim: "God is most glorified in us when we are most satisfied with Him."[4]

Through honest integrity of scientific observation, my

scientific studies revealed to me the omnipotence of God, which I could not deny. These observations motivated me to get to know this amazing Creator God, whose awesome power was starkly evident under the microscope. Once I connected with Him on a personal level, experiencing His love for me, I was filled with a life-passion to know Him better.

My motivation to know God and my lifelong pursuit to rest in His redemption was inspired through my scientific studies. The majesty of creation that I viewed under the microscope was so beyond human philosophy, evolutionary dogma, or any natural explanation that my scientific mind was humbled to acknowledge the existence of a divine Creator.

Your motivation to know God may come from another source. Many people come to God because of unbearable grief, sorrow, or other kinds of trouble for which there is no relief or human solution. In God's presence, they find the comfort and wisdom they need to carry on in life.

GOD'S LOVE IS CONTINUALLY FLOWING OUT TO DRAW LOST SOULS TO HIS WONDROUS REDEMPTION.

Some come to know God through loving friends or family, whose caring hearts they desire to emulate. When they discover that the source of their friend's love is the love of God, they are inspired to seek God for themselves. Everyone who knows God has a testimony of how God drew his or her heart to Himself. Indeed, the Holy Spirit is always working through many different avenues to reveal Jesus to needy, hurting hearts.

Churches that preach the true gospel, ministers who share the love of God through song, fellow believers who allow the love of God to flow through them to others, even the splendor of nature—in these and many other ways, God's love is continually flowing out to draw lost souls to His wondrous redemption.

KNOWING CHRIST VS. KNOWING ABOUT HIM

In my spiritual journey, I have learned that there is a great difference between knowing *about* Christ and truly abiding in Him. Jesus declared: "I am the way, the truth, and the life" (John 14:6). He taught that by believing in Him we will find life. Faith, that deeply personal spiritual conviction, is the key to receiving the atonement of Christ and learning to live in intimate relationship with Him.

Personal spiritual conviction (faith) motivates us to walk with Him as the *way*, to learn of Him as the *truth*, and to live in Him who is *life*. This personal, living relationship is much more profound than a mere mental assent to doctrines of the church. Knowing Him intimately transcends the idea of knowing *about* Him.

The good news is that God gives to every person a measure of faith to truly know Christ (Rom. 12:3). I mentioned the revelation of the apostle Paul: "By grace are ye saved through faith; and that not of yourselves: it is the gift of God: not of works, lest any man should boast" (Eph. 2:8–9). According to the Scriptures, salvation is a "free gift" (Rom. 5:16).

The apostle Paul explains, "For the wages of sin is death; but the *gift of God* is eternal life through Jesus Christ our Lord" (Rom. 6:23, emphasis added). That wonderful gift of redemption from sin is available to all who will call on the name of the Lord (Acts 2:21). That makes the mystery of divine romance with our Maker available to all who simply ask.

Jesus taught that eternal life means knowing the one true God (John 17:3). Imagine entering into that divine quality of eternal life while still living on this troubled, chaotic earth. That is what is available to us as we pursue relationship with our Redeemer through faith. Such deep personal conviction lays hold on this spiritual reality and transforms our lives day by day.

> **JESUS TAUGHT THAT ETERNAL LIFE MEANS KNOWING THE ONE TRUE GOD (JOHN 17: 3).**

Since faith to receive Christ is a gift of God, no one can argue that they just don't have the faith to believe in Him or to truly know Him. God's love transcends every excuse and fear that people have regarding the gift of redemption through Christ. The greatest moment in the life of any person is when they humble themselves to come to Christ and ask for His forgiveness. From that moment on, they begin to live as they were meant to live, justified by faith in God's eyes and receiving His peace (Rom. 5:1).

FAITH THAT CHANGES THE WORLD

When our faith is based in deep spiritual conviction, it will not be changed or diminished by our circumstances or the world we live in; rather, our faith will help us to change the world. There are spiritual giants in history who have proved this principle again and again.

William Penn, founder of Pennsylvania, was born into nobility in 1644 in London, England. His father, Sir William Penn, was an admiral who had fought with distinction the fleets of Holland and Spain. As a youth, William was educated in Oxford but was at odds with the traditional faith of his father and the practices of the Anglican "state" church. Instead, William Penn sought to know the truth of the authentic Christian message rather than institutional religion.

While at Oxford, he went to hear Thomas Loe, a Quaker preacher, who began his message with these words: "There is a faith that overcomes the world, and there is a faith that is overcome by the world." To his father's dismay, William Penn, upon hearing this message of the gospel, was converted to a personal faith in Christ. He determined that his faith would help him change the world. Little did he realize how true that would be.[5]

Early on, William Penn concluded that "true religion does not draw men out of the world but enables them to live better in it and excites their endeavors to mend it."[6] That abandonment to his personal faith in Christ motivated him to make a difference in the lives of people for the rest of his life.

So radical did William Penn become in his personal faith in Christ, teaching biblical truths, and writing pamphlets that contradicted the legitimacy of the institutionalized religion of the Anglican church, that he was thrown into the London Tower. There he lay, a prisoner, for nearly nine months. He vowed to die there rather than recant from his "conscience that I owe to no mortal man."[7] The British government finally tired of such strong resistance and released their prisoner.

"A Holy Experiment"

Then Penn's fortunes changed providentially. In payment of a debt to William's father, King Charles II gave William Penn a New World colony across the ocean. King Charles thought his shrewd offer was of dual benefit: he rid himself of an honorable debt to the navy while ridding England of this young radical leader of a "religious sect" who insisted on contradicting the legitimacy of the Anglican church.

The tract of land Penn received covered the whole of what he named Pennsylvania. There, he began what he called his "holy experiment" in forming the government of his New World colony. Its capital city he called Philadelphia, "the city of brotherly love." His frame of government for Pennsylvania set forth a representative form of government with freedom of religion for all, a penal system designed to reform not just punish, and public education available for all children. He designed Philadelphia and other towns with a grid pattern of streets, buildings, and public squares to promote health and fire safety. Thomas Jefferson called Penn "the greatest law-giver the world has produced."[8]

William Penn's faith filled him with a desire to "get it right" regarding government, living as God intended mankind to live and love and dwell in peace together. His deep spiritual conviction changed his world (and ours), laying foundational principles for governing, which would later be melded into the Constitution of the United States of America.

Penn's covenant love for God through his intimate relationship with his Creator-Redeemer led him to establish godly governing principles that would eventually influence entire nations. Through his "holy experiment," though not perfect, William Penn's faith overcame the world of institutional religion in which he had been born.

FAITH IN COVENANT LOVE

William Penn's initial conversion experience ushered him into a covenant love relationship with God. Receiving the atonement of Christ through faith is the beginning of that relationship of covenant love with the Lord that will lead the believer into consummate rest in His redemption. The supernatural love, peace, and joy that God gives fills the believer's heart with a passion to know Him more, to love Him more, and to glorify Him in everything they do. And it causes their faith to overcome the world rather than be overcome by the world.

> THERE IS A FAITH THAT OVERCOMES THE WORLD, AND THERE IS A FAITH THAT IS OVERCOME BY THE WORLD.
>
> —THOMAS LOE

Jean-Pierre de Caussade described the characteristics of this deep spiritual conviction, which is faith:

> Faith lifts and expands the heart above and beyond all that the senses fear. The life of faith and the instinct of faith are one and the same thing. It is delight in the friendship of God and confidence in his protection, which makes everything acceptable and to be received with good grace. Faith also produces a certain detachment of soul, which enables us to handle any situation and every kind of person. With faith we are never unhappy and never weak. The soul, with its living faith in God, always sees him acting behind happenings which bewilder our senses.... The robust voice of faith instantly replies: "Hold fast, go forward and fear nothing."[9]

As you cultivate this covenant relationship with your Savior, He will show you how to be effectively involved in meaningful life pursuits of family, career, and many other worthwhile things. When you choose to pursue intimate relationship with your Redeemer, learning to rest in His redemption above all else, life's involvements will become prioritized around this wonderful mystery of divine romance you enjoy with your Lord.

Legitimate, God-given pursuits will become more effective as you pursue a covenant love relationship with your Lord. The more love you receive from Him, the more you will desire to return that love in worship to Him and in fruitful service to others. And your faith will "lift and expand the heart" so that you will lay aside some otherwise harmless pursuits that do not contribute to your pursuit of life in God. Your focus will be to fulfill the purpose God reveals to you as you continually commune with your Lord.

The apostle Paul uses the analogy of marriage to describe a believer's relationship to Christ. He tells husbands to love their wives "even as Christ also loved the church, and gave himself for it" (Eph. 5:25). He declares that Christ cherishes the church. To *cherish* (*thalpo* in the Greek) means "to foster with tender, loving care."[10] That is a description of covenant love between a man and woman in marriage.

Then Paul explains that as believers we are united to Christ in a similar way. He describes this mystery of covenant relationship in terms of our becoming "members of his body, of his flesh, and of his bones" (Eph. 5:30). That does not denote a casual, intellectual relationship with our Lord. It is a spiritual relationship involving personal commitment by the two parties involved. And it results in deep, satisfying intimacy of heart and mind that involves every issue of life.

Knowing our Creator-Redeemer means our entire being is consummated in His love, in that mystery of divine romance. In our great imperfection, we have been united with divine perfection. In our poverty, we have been made partaker of the divine riches our Savior provides for us.

Consider the story of a poor country girl who marries a well-to-do, educated, sophisticated young man. They are deeply in love, united with a common respect for each other and for their goals for life. But one partner brings much more "wealth" to the relationship than the other. Immediately, after they are married, this girl who was raised in poverty becomes the owner of a beautiful home, drives an expensive car, and enjoys financial security she has never known.

KNOWING OUR CREATOR-REDEEMER MEANS OUR ENTIRE BEING IS CONSUM-MATED IN HIS LOVE.

That is a picture of the security we have when we abandon ourselves to Christ. By faith, He leads us into resting in His redemption and enjoying the wealth of His supernatural lifestyle. The apostle Paul referred to this as "Christ in you, the hope of glory" (Col. 1:27).

Through abandoning ourselves to Christ in covenant relationship, we are sure to inherit the righteous living and victorious lifestyle that He has provided for us. It is very important that we not just enter into a "dating" relationship with Christ, flirting with His promises without making a complete commitment of our lives to resting in His redemption.

Even in the Old Testament, God proclaimed Himself to be the husband of His people:

> Fear not; for thou shalt not be ashamed....For thy Maker is thine husband; the LORD of hosts is his name;

and thy Redeemer the Holy One of Israel; the God of the whole earth shall he be called.

—ISAIAH 54:4–5

Earlier, we discussed the sad reality that an entire generation of Israelites died in the wilderness because they refused to abandon themselves in faith to God's promise. That peril of self-destruction is no less real for New Testament hearers who refuse to pursue intimate relationship of resting in Christ's redemption. The writer to the Hebrew church reminds believers of Israel's failure and warns us:

> Take heed, brethren, lest there be in any of you an evil heart of unbelief, in departing from the living God....With whom was he [God] grieved forty years? was it not with them that had sinned, whose carcasses fell in the wilderness? And to whom sware he that they should not enter into his rest, but to them that believed not? So we see that they could not enter in because of unbelief.
>
> —HEBREWS 3:12, 17–19

How sad that the generation who had seen the power of God in Egypt ultimately refused to enter into His rest. They failed to enter their Promised Land. They did not change the world through their faith; their faith instead was diminished because of their fear of the world.

Their lack of trust in God to empower them to conquer the giants of the land, as He had promised to do, resulted in their wasting their lives wandering in the wilderness—and dying there. These Israelites did not mix the Word of God with their faith, so it did not profit them (Heb. 4:2). As a result, God refused to let them enter into His rest (Heb. 3:10–11).

As we submit our lives to God, our faith will bring us into God's rest: "For we which have believed do enter into rest" (Heb. 4:3). When we enter into His rest, we cease from our own works, as God did from His (v. 10). When we allow Christ to become our righteousness, we learn to enjoy His spiritual rest in all of life.

Our priority as believers is to "be zealous and exert ourselves and strive diligently to enter into that rest [of God, to know and experience it for ourselves], that no one may fall or perish by the same kind of unbelief and disobedience [into which those in the wilderness fell]" (Heb. 4:11, AMP). Faith is the key to living fruitful lives and enjoying God's promises. When some asked Jesus what they had to do to work the works of God, Jesus declared:

> HAVE YOU CONSIDERED *BELIEVING GOD* TO BE YOUR SUPREME LIFE WORK?

This is the work of God, that ye believe on him whom he hath sent.

—JOHN 6:29

Have you considered *believing God* to be your supreme life work? What about believing the wonderful promises of God and entering into the divine romance of walking with the Savior? What about resting in His redemption? The more we commune with God, the closer we come to the purpose for which we were created: to glorify God in all we do and enjoy Him forever.

FAITH AND WORKS

As we saw in the life of William Penn, who was willing to suffer persecution for his faith in Christ, God opened effective opportunities for him to change the world. Unless we pursue intimate relationship with God according to His Word, we will inevitably try to do good works that ultimately bring glory to ourselves. The Scriptures show us how to fulfill the real purpose of God for our lives:

> Be renewed in the spirit of your mind; and that ye put on the new man, which after God is created in righteousness and true holiness.
>
> —EPHESIANS 4:23–24

Without faith, it is impossible to please God (Heb. 11:6). As we enter into the rest of His redemption, our faith will believe His promises: "For he that cometh to God must believe that he is, and that he is a rewarder of them that diligently seek him" (Heb. 11:6).

It is clear throughout the Scriptures that our primary goal in life must be to seek God in faith, to know Him, and to abandon our lives to the mystery of that divine romance. Jesus taught us to live with this priority:

> "You must love the Lord your God with all your heart, all your soul, and all your mind." This is the first and greatest commandment. A second is equally important: "Love your neighbor as yourself." The entire law and all the demands of the prophets are based on these two commandments.
>
> —MATTHEW 22:37–40, NLT

As we learn to abide in Christ, everything we do will be guided by our passionate love to fulfill the purpose of God in our lives. Jesus said, "My sheep hear my voice, and I know them, and they follow me: and I give unto them eternal life; and they shall never perish, neither shall any man pluck them out of my hand" (John 10:27–28).

> **OUR VOCATION IS THE LOVE OF JESUS.**
> —MOTHER TERESA

Until we have cultivated this intimate relationship with Christ, we cannot hear His voice or be led by the Spirit of God. Our focus must be first on abiding in Him, and then He will lead us into the good works He has ordained for us to walk in.

> For by grace are ye saved through faith; and that not of yourselves: it is the gift of God: not of works, lest any man should boast. For we are his workmanship, created in Christ Jesus unto good works, which God hath before ordained that we should walk in them.
> —EPHESIANS 2:8–10

Even when we know we are doing the work God has given us to do, we must continue to focus on our relationship with Him. Otherwise, we will find ourselves consumed with the *work* of the Lord to the neglect of the *Lord* of the work. That is a recipe for disaster. Mother Teresa observed:

> There is always the danger that we may just do the work for the sake of the work. This is where the respect and the love and the devotion come in—that we do it to God, to Christ, and that's why we try to do it as beautifully as possible.[11]

Also, she said:

> Many people mistake our work for our vocation. Our vocation is the love of Jesus.[12]

"Our vocation is the love of Jesus." I have been guilty of losing that focus at times in pursuing my personal vocation. Have you? I have become so busy with my medical practice and other responsibilities of family, church, and so on, that I forfeit all rest, even physical rest. When I was an intern, there were many times when I had very little sleep for days. Even when I tried to sleep, I was unable to rest because I was so "tuned out" to resting.

We miss so much of life as our Lord intended it when we allow our life activities and involvements to spiral out of control. Not only do our bodies suffer, but also we lose the sense of God's presence in our lives when we fail to enjoy the rest for our souls that He offers us.

I have learned that the heavier my workload—the greater the stress of demands on my time and energies—the more I need to turn off my worries and totally rest in His redemption. As I consciously focus on my relationship with Christ and His promises to be there for me, I have found that things get better. I rely on His strength in me to accomplish the tasks at hand. Instead of working harder, I concentrate on resting harder and leaning on Him. Jesus promised that if we would simply come to Him we would find rest for our souls (Matt. 11:28). John Wesley, early founder of the Methodist Church, said: "I have so much to do that I spend several hours in prayer before I am able to do it."[13]

I had a mentor who used to say that he would pray longer

on the days that he had more work to do. Instead of getting up earlier and working longer, he would pray longer. He knew he could not do anything without Jesus. So he began his prayer time by thanking God for planning all of creation, expressing gratitude for Christ's incarnation of becoming man and providing our redemption. He thanked Him for imputing His righteousness to us and making possible the consummation of our love for Him. He could feel his mind relax and his perspective change when he focused in this way on his relationship with God. And he would walk through his day in the strength of the Lord.

The essence of Christianity is that we learn to rest in His grace, His love, His Person, and His redemption. To live in that reality, we must learn not to rest in our own accomplishments, abilities, or intellectual conclusions about life. Instead, we focus on the One who cares for our eternal souls and has provided all we need to live victoriously.

Then, when challenges, injustices, hurts, and trials come, we know the source of our life. We can turn to Him for wisdom, comfort, grace to forgive, and the ability to love others the way He loves us. That is the benefit of living every moment in dependency on our Redeemer.

CONSEQUENCES OF UNBELIEF

If we choose not to abide in Christ and not to rest in His redemption through intimate fellowship with Him, we will often find ourselves plagued by many kinds of sins, especially the destructive sin of *worry*. In my book R_X *for Worry*, I explain:

> Chronic worry creates destructive anxiety and stress in our lives. It destroys our relationship with God and other people. When we embrace the negative mind-set of worry, we accuse others, judge others, discourage others, and try to control others. We're negative people who don't feel God's love and can't love others. But when we have a thankful spirit, God's peace and love fill our lives. Our focus is on His eternal presence and blessings. We are positive, trusting, loving, supportive, and appreciative.[14]

Many people confess to be Christians and have a good knowledge of theology, yet they live in continual distress, worry, and anxiety. They are missing the essence of Christianity. They do not enjoy the mystery of intimate relationship with God through faith in Christ.

According to the Scriptures, "[mere] knowledge causes people to be puffed up (to bear themselves loftily and be proud), but love (affection and benevolence and goodwill) edifies and builds up and encourages one to grow [to his full stature]" (1 Cor. 8:1, AMP).

Avoid "lukewarmness" at all costs.

One of the saddest scriptures in the entire Bible describes God's attitude against those who do not abandon themselves completely to His love and fully obey His will. When Jesus revealed Himself to John on the isle of Patmos, He gave him a message to give to the churches. To the church of the Laodiceans, He told John to write:

> These things saith the Amen, the faithful and true witness, the beginning of the creation of God; I know thy works, that thou art neither cold nor hot: I would thou

wert cold or hot. So then because thou art lukewarm, and neither cold nor hot, I will spue thee out of my mouth.

—REVELATION 3:14–16

The condition of this church was less than desirable in the sight of God; He could not tolerate their lack of commitment. He tells them they are utterly deceived in who they think they are. They say they are rich and don't need anything; they don't know they are "wretched, and miserable, and poor, and blind, and naked" (v. 17).

The word *lukewarm* literally means "tepid" or "warm." The Greek word, *chilaros,* used metaphorically, refers to the condition of a soul wretchedly fluctuating between a torpor (lethargy, extreme sluggishness) and a fervor of love.[15] According to *Vine's Dictionary,* the word was used here to show that the Laodicean church afforded no refreshment to the Lord such as He would receive from either cold or hot water.[16]

Lukewarm. Who can stand it? Coffee is meant to be a tantalizingly hot beverage, and iced tea to be deliciously cold. If either becomes lukewarm, we readily understand the urge to spew it out. Yet, as Christians, if we are honest with ourselves, we must admit that we can fall into this lukewarm category in our walk with God—mentally and spiritually sluggish, lethargic in regard to our relationship with the Lord, and offering a halfhearted focus on His will for our lives. We are tempted to fill our lives with perceived riches, not realizing how bankrupt our souls have become.

Evidently, Christ holds out more hope for those who are still "cold" to His love and redemption. He knows that these souls will warm to His love when they become aware of the blessing of His redemption for their lives. They will respond in the heat of passionate love to His forgiveness and cleansing. Many will learn to enjoy His presence in intimate communion with Him and to pursue His destiny for their lives.

Of course, believers who are "hot" are continually pursuing the mysteries of divine romance with their lovely Lord. They can't get enough of His Word, communion with Him in prayer, fellowship with the saints, or greater abandonment to His divine destiny for their lives.

It is those who have tasted of His redemption but have turned to earthly pleasures or been consumed by worries and cares of this life that God refers to as lukewarm. Yet even if we find ourselves identified with these poor creatures, God holds out to us His redemptive hope:

> I counsel thee to buy of me gold tried in the fire, that thou mayest be rich; and white raiment, that thou mayest be clothed, and that the shame of thy nakedness do not appear; and anoint thine eyes with eyesalve, that thou mayest see. As many as I love, I rebuke and chasten; be zealous therefore, and repent.
> —REVELATION 3:18–19

According to the Scriptures, it is possible for any of us to slip into a lukewarm state in our walk with God without being aware of it. The Scriptures clearly state that this church did not know their wretched state. It is imperative that we guard against lukewarmness and follow the remedy Christ gave for this condition if we find ourselves losing the fire of our love-pursuit of God.

In the Scriptures, gold is a picture of godly character and white raiment of purity. The lukewarm believer is admonished to receive God's divine counsel and to seek gold from Him—His character—and white raiment—His purity of heart. If we find ourselves in a lukewarm condition, we should determine to receive the eye salve of His Word that renews our minds to behold the truth. We need to repent and turn from our casual ways that do not reflect a hot pursuit of God Himself.

Only by abandoning ourselves to God can we avoid the trap of lukewarmness in our Christian lives. Only by continually receiving His love can we avoid living a life of fear and anxiety to enjoy the peace He promises. Otherwise we risk living our lives bound by a "spirit of infirmity" that can cripple our entire being—body, soul, and spirit.

GUARDING AGAINST THE SPIRIT OF INFIRMITY

Jesus was teaching in the synagogue one day and saw a woman who had been bowed over for eighteen years with a spirit of infirmity and "could in no wise lift up herself" (Luke 13:11). He called her to Himself and said to her, "Woman, thou art loosed from thine infirmity" (v. 12). When Jesus laid His hands on her, she stood up straight and praised God.

The word for *infirmity* Jesus used refers to both physical and spiritual sickness: "weakness of body and soul; lack of strength to bear trials and troubles; frailty."[17] Here it seems Jesus was speaking to the woman's spiritual condition as well as her physical ailment. Her soul was sick, and her body was crippled. Jesus loosed her from her spiritual bondage and healed her body.

Matthew's Gospel declared this dual power of redemption for our soul and body that Jesus brought to mankind:

> When the even was come, they brought unto him many that were possessed with devils: and he cast out the spirits with his word, and healed all that were sick: that it might be fulfilled which was spoken by Esaias the prophet, saying, Himself took our infirmities, and bare our sicknesses.
>
> —MATTHEW 8:16–17

Matthew was quoting from Isaiah, who said, "Surely he has born our griefs, and carried our sorrows...and with his stripes we are healed" (Isa. 53:4–5). The Hebrew word for "griefs" is also translated *sickness*, whether internal or external (Strong's H2483). These and other biblical references to our infirmities point to the bondage of our sin-sick souls as well as to our physical illnesses, all of which Jesus came to heal.

Medical science has more recently confirmed that our mental outlook and our emotional states (which are aspects of our soul) have an impact on our physical bodies. For example, worry is a progressive disease that can ruin our lives and even kill us. It has tangible effects on our physical health and depletes our emotional well-being. Worry can destroy our ability to fight against disease by decreasing our natural immunity. Our decreased immunity permits common colds to strike us, and if our immune system breaks down further, worry may even cause us to be stricken by more serious diseases.[18]

Anxiety has been cited as the basis for many psychiatric diseases as well. Charles Mayo, cofounder of the Mayo Clinic, pointed out how worry affects the body. It can wreak havoc with the circulatory system, the heart, the glands, and the nervous system, to name just a few. Mayo used to say that he never knew anybody who died of overwork, but he did know people who died of worry.[19]

I tell my patients that my greatest sin of commission is worry; my greatest sin of omission is *lack of appreciation*. We can worry ourselves to death, but we can never worry ourselves into a longer, healthier, happier life. In contrast, when we are filled with a spirit of thanksgiving, we are at peace with God and can live our lives resting in His redemption.

Consider this very realistic scenario. A patient received a diagnosis of glaucoma from her ophthalmologist. Although she was a Christian, she was a typically anxious person, cringing before life's challenges in fear, failing to trust God for His peace and not resting in His redemption. She did not know that her particular diagnosis was the type that would never cause any significant harm to her sight, as is the case in about one-third of glaucoma diagnoses.

When this anxious patient heard the diagnosis, she immediately began worrying about the devastating effects it would have on her life. She was so preoccupied with her concern that it interfered with her enjoyment of life, her daily routines, her relationships, and her work. At the beginning, she suffered only moderate worry, wondering how she would deal with the looming disease that could destroy her eyesight. As time went by, she became so obsessed with constant worry about this diagnosis that there was no room left for positive thoughts of wellness, optimism for a favorable outcome, or other positive considerations.

As a result of her obsession with worry, her prayer life suffered. Her ability to worship her Creator was blocked out by the power of anxiety. She lost the passion she once had to identify herself as a child of her Creator-Redeemer. It was then that she began noticing pains in her joints and muscles; she was depressed and tired, suffering an acute inability to concentrate. Her memory became less functional as well. As her depression deepened, her desire to be with others decreased and she withdrew from relationships. Her life was so self-absorbed in her mind-set of constant worry that she lost interest and motivation to do the things she had once enjoyed doing.

As the worry became more prominent, she began to choose "comfort foods" over more nutritional ones. She gorged on foods that tasted good but did not provide her body with energy. She began to gain weight and, because the pancreas cannot control sugar levels over a healthy weight, she became diabetic. The more apparent her systemic diseases became, the less she exercised, which also compromised her general health.

Not surprisingly, the health of this patient, who was "crippled" with worry over a diagnosis that would not necessarily have affected her sight, went steadily downhill. She developed hypertension, which led to more serious health problems.

Admittedly this is an extreme case of a woman who gave in to a spirit of infirmity, allowing the worrying spirit to consume her. However, we all need to be cautious that we do not entertain such destructive attitudes in the face of serious life challenges.

It is important to determine where you might be on the spectrum of destructive mind-sets that begin with just a little worry and mistrust and can lead to life-threatening conditions like I described above. Some patients become so overwhelmed with their negative mind-sets that they have to be institutionalized or become bedridden patients, suffering premature deaths.

Every day, as we treat people at St. Luke's Cataract and Laser Institute, we encounter troubled souls who are extremely worried about their physical condition. Perhaps they suffer with Fuchs' dystrophy, keratoconus, glaucoma, macular degeneration, or another serious eye condition. But many have given in to a spirit of infirmity that affects their internal health as well and needs to be treated as certainly as an infection or cancer.

Such "infirmities" of the soul need to be dealt with in a sensitive and understanding way, rather than just telling a person to "buck up" or get a grip on life. Graciously and kindly, we must find a way to talk with our patients about their negative attitude and mind-set and how it can affect their physical health.

In just a few minutes, I can relate to my patients my personal struggle with overcoming worry. I tell them it is one of my worst sins. I relate the possible effects it can have on their spiritual and physical health, and I contrast it with the power of filling their mind and heart with thanksgiving and praise to God. Often the immediate release these words bring to a patient is pronounced as they gain understanding to see the effects of the spirit of infirmity on their minds; they begin to think rationally and become filled with hope for a different outcome.

When Jesus loosed the woman from a spirit of infirmity, Scripture says she stood up straight and began to praise God. Praising God is always the healthy response to the goodness of God as we confront the challenges of life. The apostle Paul, with good reason, exhorted all believers in the proper way to think:

> Always be full of joy in the Lord. I say it again—
> rejoice!…Don't worry about anything; instead, pray
> about everything. Tell God what you need, and thank
> him for all he has done. Then you will experience God's
> peace, which exceeds anything we can understand.…Fix
> your thoughts on what is true, and honorable, and right,
> and pure, and lovely, and admirable. Think about things
> that are excellent and worthy of praise.
> —Philippians 4:4, 6–7, 8, NLT

Life will present frightening challenges to every person who lives on this planet. It is in the way we choose to confront them that will determine a negative or positive outcome for our lives. The apostle Paul on one occasion listed the many trials and tribulations he had faced to that point in his life—beatings, imprisonments, shipwreck, robbers, and dangers in city, desert, and on the sea.

He also suffered the effects of a "thorn in the flesh" meant to keep him humble in light of the great revelation he had received from God (2 Cor. 12:7). When he begged the Lord to take it away, Jesus spoke to him: "My grace is sufficient for thee: for my strength is made perfect in weakness" (v. 9). So Paul received the grace of God for his troublesome situation and showed us the proper attitude we must all have in our distressful situations: "Therefore I take pleasure in infirmities, in reproaches, in necessities, in persecutions, in distresses for Christ's sake; for when I am weak, then am I strong" (v. 10).

Even when we do not see deliverance from our present troubles, we do not have to give in to a spirit of infirmity that cripples our mind and our emotions and has the power to destroy our body. We simply receive the strength of Christ in our weakness and are filled with His love and grace—resting in His redemption. So powerful is this divine strength in the soul that Paul said, "Most gladly therefore will I rather glory in my infirmities, that the power of Christ may rest upon me" (v. 9). There it is—*grace*. That supernatural charisma that dispels our darkness, delivers us from bondage, and turns suffering into glory; it is the mystery of redemption that causes us to walk in His divine light, freedom, and love.

Rather than bringing us into bondage, our weaknesses and difficulties should be catalysts to enter more deeply into the mystery of divine romance with our Lord. They should become opportunities to experience the power of Christ resting upon us; we don't have to give in to a spirit of infirmity that entertains pessimistic thoughts of defeat, destruction, and death. His grace is sufficient to make us victorious Christians, filled with fervent love, genuine thanksgiving, and the peace and joy of resting in His redemption.

It is unfortunate that many Christians suffer from a lack of this knowledge of Christ's delivering power, which leaves them to suffer the effects of a spirit of infirmity in soul and body. These divine mysteries of the power of Christ's redemption are not always understood, much less practiced, even by Christian leaders who are trying to guide others into Christ's redemption.

Anxious theologians

There are Christian leaders who have given their lives to study theology, which means literally "the study of religious faith, practice, and experience; especially: the study of God and of God's relation to the world."[20] They can give eloquent speeches and write lengthy treatises on doctrines they have formulated based on the Scriptures. They become so absorbed in their viewpoint and so convinced of its prowess that they worry over every criticism or the different points of view of others. In short, they forfeit the peace of God for their scholarly conclusions and their theological viewpoints.

Of course, an understanding of basic theological concepts is absolutely essential for the believer who wants to enjoy a covenant relationship with God. We must cultivate an informed mind so that we base our relationship with God on sound theology. However, that informed mind should give way to an inflamed heart filled with passion and gratitude to our Lord and Creator who has shown us the way to be restored by resting in His redemption.

Intricate theological interpretation of difficult passages should never take precedence over the truth of divine relationship. It should not be allowed to circumvent our rest in our Savior's redemption. The motivation of theologians may be to gain knowledge for the purpose of personal recognition, self-glorification, or other equally selfish reasons. They can write all the books in the world about Christianity. But unless they learn to rest by faith in His redemption, these anxious theologians will not experience the peace of God and His power to love others.

In contrast, an inflamed heart of love for the Master will lead to engaged hands that determine to glorify God in all they do. This is our proper orientation to theology. It is also the correct perspective for relating to the people in our lives, to our vocation, to our pursuit of justice, and to every challenge of life.

This perspective of life will remove anxiety, personal opinion, and mere intellectual assent to doctrine. Living to glorify God and to enjoy Him will result in the peace, joy, and righteousness that are dependent on vibrant communion with our Redeemer. Any other priority, no matter how noble, will ultimately keep us from entering into the rest of God. It will surely bring defeat to our lives.

"Defeated" Christian workers

You probably know of someone who had genuine aspirations to serve God in a full-time vocation but failed to realize their life goals. Instead, disappointed and sometimes disillusioned, they opted to enter a secular field of work. Sadly, that is a growing trend among Christian leaders.

According to national data on the state of pastors in North America, the following statistics confirm that many Christian leaders are suffering frustration, anxiety, and discouragement that ultimately defeat their goals for ministry:

- Nationally, 1,500 pastors leave the ministry each month due to burnout, moral failure, or conflict in the church. That's 18,000 per year!
- Of those who begin in the ministry, 50 percent leave after their first pastorate in less than five years, never to return to ministry though they felt called.
- Only 10 percent finish the race and reach age sixty-five as a pastor.
- Of pastors' spouses, 80 percent wish their spouse would choose another profession.[21]

This same study found that two-thirds of these pastors reported conflict among their congregation for at least two years. And 90 percent concluded that their seminary training did not prepare them for the realities of day-to-day life as a Christian leader. In spite of their knowledge of theology, these pastors were not equipped with the reality of learning to rest in Christ's redemption.

No personal rest; no peace; no loving support from their denominational leaders, their friends, or their parishioners. This sad picture that affects scores of churches and Christian leaders underscores the devastating effects of faulty "theology."

It's clear that knowledge *about* Christ did not lead these leaders by faith into intimate relationship with Him. They did not grasp the wondrous mystery of being "in Christ" (Col. 1:2, 28) or of "Christ in [us], the hope of glory" (Col. 1:27). Without walking in that truth, they could not make relationship with God their first vocation.

In an article titled "Effective Christian Leadership: Vocation vs. Occupation," Stevan Becker, president and trustee of Christians in Commerce, concludes: "The problem with our society today isn't that it doesn't know that God exists. In fact, survey after survey reveals that more than eighty percent of our citizenry believe in God's existence. *The problem is that we live as if he doesn't exist.*" Becker explains:

> Paul identifies this fundamental sin against God as impiety (read Rom. 1:18–23), the refusal to acknowledge God and his rightful place in our lives. We violate God's divine rights as creator. This is the sin that drives all our self-centeredness and the resulting problems in our lives and society.... The resulting sin is killing us and our fellow workers. Destroying our lives. Creating greater problems, hurting our families, our society, alienating us from each other, filling us with bitterness and resentment, lust and avarice. Jesus wants to use us to rescue

others from their sin and bring them into the fullness of their created purpose and therefore into his Kingdom.[22]

Only as we learn to rest in God's redemption—in whatever vocation we choose—will that divine relationship direct our priorities for success. We'll understand that our divine romance with God will permeate our actions and attitudes in such a way that everyone around us will benefit from His love.

Becker explains: "Seeing our occupation as a part of our real vocation is the kingdom perspective. Work is faithful stewardship of one area of influence and authority that has been trusted into our care. It's integrated into my life. My focus is not on acquiring or accomplishing but obeying God's will."[23]

LISTEN TO YOUR WORDS

To know if your faith in Christ is leading you into obedience to His kingdom purpose, listen to your words. What are you speaking? Are you focused on your own misgivings, fears, and worries? Your personal success? Are you speaking doubt and worry words?

What are you listening to? Are you receiving false or humanistic teaching that denies the supernatural dimension of a relationship with Christ? Or is your priority to embrace the promises of the Word of God and speaking to yourself its truths? The apostle Paul admonishes us:

LISTENING TO, SPEAKING, AND BELIEVING THE WORD OF GOD WILL RESTORE PEACE AND JOY TO OUR SOULS.

> Wherefore be ye not unwise, but understanding what
> the will of the Lord is. And be not drunk with wine,
> wherein is excess; but be filled with the Spirit; speaking
> to yourselves in psalms and hymns and spiritual songs,
> singing and making melody in your heart to the Lord;
> giving thanks always for all things unto God and the
> Father in the name of our Lord Jesus Christ.
> —EPHESIANS 5:17–20

The Scriptures have much to say about the power of our words. Paul taught that we must not listen to everything that is spoken, even in the name of church doctrine, but that "speaking the truth in love," we will grow into mature Christians (Eph. 4:15). He said we must put off our former kinds of conversation, which was corrupt. Instead, we must "be renewed in the spirit of [our] mind" (Eph. 4:23). Listening to, speaking, and believing the Word of God will restore the peace and joy to our souls that Christ's redemption provides.

Until I abandon myself by faith to the mystery of divine romance with my Savior, I will not fulfill the purpose of the Scriptures for my life. I will be condemned to living in wearisome self-effort, following rules and gritting my teeth to live peaceably with others. It is this mystery of a love relationship with Christ that sets me free to rest in His redemption. He flows His divine love through my mind and heart for every situation.

Established by faith in Him, I am protected from the peril of unbelief and led into divine purpose for my life. And as I listen to His redemptive Word, I speak in faith what He gives me to speak.

DISCOVERING PURPOSE FOR LIFE

Earlier we saw that William Penn discovered his purpose for life through His covenant relationship with Christ that secured his faith. I love what Paul teaches believers about discovering purpose for life:

> God saved you by his grace when you believed. And you can't take credit for this; it is a gift from God. Salvation is not a reward for the good things we have done, so none of us can boast about it. For we are God's masterpiece. He has created us anew in Christ Jesus, so that we can do the good things he planned for us long ago.
>
> —EPHESIANS 2:8–10, NLT

Such clarity in the Scriptures should erase any misconception of our needing to work for our salvation; salvation is a gift from God. We can't take credit for it or boast about it in any way. But after salvation, we learn why we were created anew: to be God's masterpieces, redeemed so that we can fulfill His purpose for us that He planned a long time ago.

What an incredible thought! The yearning I have to live a purposeful life was put into my heart by God Himself!

THE YEARNING I HAVE TO LIVE A PURPOSEFUL LIFE WAS PUT INTO MY HEART BY GOD HIMSELF.

And it is in abandoning myself to His gift of redemption that I will discover the good things He purposed for me to do. They will satisfy that yearning of my heart to enjoy God and glorify Him in all I do.

Satisfying true soul hunger

Richard Leider is ranked by *Forbes* as one of the top five most respected executive coaches. He coauthored with David Shapiro a book called *Something to Live For.* These astute authors concluded that there are three hungers people try to feed throughout their lives:

1. To connect deeply with the creative spirit of life

2. To know and express our gifts and talents

3. To know that our lives matter[24]

The human soul longs to know that there is a purpose for its existence. The futility of living life with no sense of purpose leads many into despair. In pursuing the mystery of romance with Christ, we learn that God has ordained us for a divine purpose, and He gives us grace to fulfill it. In Christ, every divine hunger of the human heart is realized. The Scriptures declare:

> And we know that all things work together for good to them that love God, to them who are the called according to his purpose.
>
> —Romans 8:28

> Now unto him that is able to keep you from falling, and to present you faultless before the presence of his glory with exceeding joy, to the only wise God our Saviour, be glory and majesty, dominion and power, both now and ever. Amen.
>
> —Jude 24–25

A missing link

I admired one of my professors who was a brilliant man. He was one of the most profound scientific thinkers I have ever met. When he died recently, his children held his funeral at a yacht club. They served alcoholic beverages and appetizers to guests who reminisced about the phenomenal achievements of their father's life.

I appreciated this real tribute to a truly great scientist's life work. But I was keenly aware that there was something missing from their eulogies. There was a missing link to the eternality of life. No one there expressed anything that spoke of eternity or the redemption of this man's soul, which the Scriptures teach is destined to live forever.

His was a brilliant life, full of adventures and noteworthy achievements in this world. He searched for truth within the molecular scientific realm through his studies. His goal was to help people, finding new treatments for disease and developing cures for their illnesses.

But it was evident from all that was said about him that his pursuit of truth ended with his noble vocation. The missing link in their comments was the lack of eternal perspective. That involves a far greater reality than scientific brilliance or humanitarianism. This revered scientist seemed to have missed the truth of eternal salvation that comes only to the soul of a man resting in God's redemption.

How tragic it is to observe this missing link in a life that is otherwise so legitimately respected. Earthly achievements will never replace the need for faith that embraces the truth that God is a rewarder of those who diligently seek Him (Heb. 11:6). Personal accomplishments can never fulfill the hunger of the human heart for rest found only in the redemption of

Christ. They can never prepare the eternal human soul to live forever with their Creator-Redeemer.

Faith Is "Standing"

Stand your ground, putting on the belt of truth and the body armor of God's righteousness.
—Ephesians 6:14, nlt

Faith, our deep personal conviction, stands on the promises of God and determines to walk in the purposes of God. You stand on your faith just as you stand on His redemption and His promises. As you focus on the greatness of His redemption, your priority in life is transformed. You do not live to please yourself or to gain personal recognition. You consider Jesus alone in everything you do. By faith, you live to please the Lord and to bring glory to His name:

And whatever you do [no matter what it is] in word or deed, do everything in the name of the Lord Jesus and in [dependence upon] His Person, giving praise to God the Father through Him.
—Colossians 3:17, amp

Living in intimate fellowship with God gives you the strength to stand firm in your faith. It is the key to fulfilling His purpose for your life.

Therefore, my beloved brethren, be ye stedfast, unmoveable, always abounding in the work of the Lord, forasmuch as ye know that your labour is not in vain in the Lord.
—1 Corinthians 15:58

As a born-again child of God, learning to walk in His purposes is a result of resting in the redemption of Christ. Fulfilling your divine destiny involves your complete abandonment to intimate relationship with Him. That love relationship is a divine mystery of covenant commitment filled with joy, peace, and contentment. It is the key to freedom from fear and worry.

LIVING IN INTIMATE FELLOWSHIP WITH GOD GIVES YOU THE STRENGTH TO STAND FIRM IN YOUR FAITH.

Learning to abide in Christ enables you to do everything you were meant to do in dependence upon His Person. When you make this divine relationship the priority of your life, you will be enlarged in your heart and mind to accomplish more than you ever dreamed possible.

PERSONAL MEDITATION

CHAPTER 3

There are many things about the creation of this earth and all of life that we do not understand. Do we simply have to leave our unanswerable questions until we get to heaven? (See 1 Corinthians 13:9–12.)

_____

_____

Does God live in your house?

_____

_____

If we remove legalism from Christianity, is Christ's redemption not its core value?

_____

_____

In Hebrew, does the word *atonement* signify that "another has taken my place—suffered the death I deserve because of my sins"?

_____

_____

Is the message of entering into spiritual rest with God the same in both Old and New Testaments?

_____

_____

We receive Christ's redemption when we are justified by faith. Does that result in peace? (See Colossians 1:20 and Romans 5:1.)

_____

_____

Can we live in peace without resting in His redemption?

_____

_____

Is worry the opposite of resting in His redemption? How does worry affect your relationship with God, yourself, and with others?

_____

_____

When we enter His rest, do we really cease from our own striving? (See Hebrews 4:1–11.)

_____

_____

This is faith: a renouncing of everything we are apt to call our own and relying wholly upon the blood, righteousness and intercession of Jesus.... Our righteousness is in Him, and our hope depends, not upon the exercise of grace in us, but upon the fullness of grace and love in Him, and upon His obedience unto death.

—JOHN NEWTON[1]

4

WALKING IN GOD'S FORGIVENESS

P ERHAPS YOU HAVE read about John Newton (1725–
1807), who may be better known for composing the
beloved hymn "Amazing Grace" than for his infamous
life as the captain of an English slave-trader ship. His own
description of his debauched life as a young man and then as
a slave trader ranks with the apostle Paul's self-description: he
called himself the "chief of sinners" (1 Tim. 1:15).

Newton's radical conversion and subsequent long years of
service as a caring pastor is a fascinating story. It is a powerful testimony to the gospel message that transforms the
lives of those who truly follow Christ. When he was an old
man, Newton exclaimed in deep gratitude: "My memory is
nearly gone; but I remember two things; that I am a great
sinner, and that Christ is a great Saviour."[2] Newton also said:

> How sweet the name of Jesus sounds in a believer's ear!
> It soothes his sorrows, heals his wounds, and drives
> away his fear.[3]

In David Jeremiah's powerful book *Captured by Grace*,
Pastor Jeremiah places John Newton's conversion story side
by side with the apostle Paul's. He shows the dramatic power

of the grace of God that captured these two decadent hearts and transformed their lives. After their conversions to Christ, their lives were as different as darkness is from light.

Pastor Jeremiah shares the words of John Newton when he explained his catalyst for finally looking heavenward. It was during a life-threatening storm at sea. After a beloved "companion in decadence" took his own place on deck and was swept overboard, Newton concluded that that deadly wave was meant for him.

> MY MEMORY IS NEARLY GONE; BUT I REMEMBER TWO THINGS; THAT I AM A GREAT SINNER, AND THAT CHRIST IS A GREAT SAVIOUR.
>
> —JOHN NEWTON

With a newly awakened sense of guilt for his life of sin, Newton began to search for a way to find faith. Remembering his mother's godly training, he searched for a Bible on the ship and began reading. His eyes fell on the verse: "If ye then, being evil, know how to give good gifts to your children: how much more shall your heavenly Father give the Holy Spirit to them that ask him?" (Luke 11:13). Newton was struck by the words, "If ye then, being evil…"

In that moment, he understood that he needed to get in touch with the Holy Spirit: "I have need of that very Spirit, by which the whole was written, in order to understand it aright," he wrote. "He has engaged here to give that Spirit to those who ask: I must therefore pray for it; and, if it be of God, He will make good on His own word."[4]

John Newton would later testify that it was in those tortuous moments that he embraced the truth of the Gospels and the power of their Savior to rescue him from the hell he had fashioned of his own life. In those pages, he found the one and only hope that could rescue him from the anguish and despair that had become his permanent dwelling place. It was hard for him to believe: all his sins, blotted out in one moment; all that was wretched about him, forgiven.

Much later, he wrote about finding his faith in Christ and entering into His peace, though he did not yet know the blissful rest he would find in his intimate relationship with Christ: "I had no apprehension of...the hidden life of a Christian, as it consists in communion with God by Jesus Christ; a continual dependence upon him."[5]

During his subsequent long life, Newton's words and actions truly reflected the divine rest and romance with God that is available to all who embrace His "amazing grace." Wonderful is the mystery of the indwelling Christ, the communion of Spirit with spirit! It is the divine romance that is waiting for the "worst" sinners who will dare to trust Him with their past, their present, and their future. That is the supernatural power of forgiveness available to those who will but ask God for it.

THE REDEEMING POWER OF FORGIVENESS

There is perhaps no other word so significant to personal freedom than the word *forgiveness*. To be truly forgiven for wrongdoing, either by God or by another human being, is the most liberating reality that the human heart can experience.

The love of God is the only source of true forgiveness. When a human heart has experienced that divine forgiveness for sin, it is empowered to extend forgiveness to others. The power to forgive is not a natural human virtue; its source is found only in the love of God flowing through a redeemed human heart.

According to Webster's dictionary, to *forgive* means "to cease to feel resentment against (an offender): pardon" and "to give up resentment of or claim to requital for."[6] That does not describe the natural reactions of our human nature. It is no wonder there is so much retaliation in the world in communities; between races, gangs, politicians; and in marriages and families. Sadly, this hostile attitude toward others can even be witnessed in our churches.

According to human standards, any perceived injustice demands *retaliation*, but God's standard response to injustice is *forgiveness*. Remember, the Bible says that God is love (1 John 4:8). He displayed the power of His love to triumph over injustice when He sacrificed His only Son, who was perfect and without sin, to die for the sins of the whole world.

The four Gospels (Matthew, Mark, Luke, and John) are filled with stories that reveal to us the loving, forgiving heart of God toward sinners. The following are examples of the wondrous mercy that flows from God's heart to sin-sick humanity. In these five passages we observe that Luke, the beloved physician, had a special eye for the lowly, broken, burdened soul:

1. In Luke chapter 7, a well-known woman with a reputation for being a sinner came to Jesus with an alabaster box of ointment, which she poured on the feet of Jesus. Weeping, she worshiped Him, while others criticized Jesus for allowing a sinner to touch him. Jesus said to them, "Her sins, which are many, are forgiven;

for she loved much: but to whom little is forgiven, the same loveth little" (v. 47).

2. In Luke chapter 15, we read the familiar story
   of the prodigal son who asked for his inheritance, left his father's house, and squandered
   it on loose living. When famine came, he
   was forced to live with pigs and eat the same
   husks they ate. When he came to his senses,
   he decided to return to his father, whom he
   had disgraced and scorned. His father ran to
   meet him, bent to embrace and kiss him, and
   celebrated his homecoming. Without retaliation for his loss, this loving father restored his
   son to dignity and authority in his home. This
   is a picture of the great heart of God for every
   sinner who returns to find rest for his soul in
   the redemption of Christ.

3. In Luke chapter 18, Jesus tells the story of a
   publican, a tax collector for the Romans, who
   went up to the temple to pray. He did not
   even look up but beat his breast in a sign of
   recognition of his unworthiness to be heard by
   God. Jesus said that his contrition was heard
   and he was justified before God. In contrast,
   a Pharisee, a religious leader of the day, stood
   beside the publican and commended his own
   righteousness. He compared himself favorably
   to the publican standing nearby. Jesus condemned the Pharisee, saying: "Every one that

exalteth himself shall be abased; and he that humbleth himself shall be exalted" (v. 14).

4. In Luke chapter 22, we encounter the conversation between Jesus and His disciple Peter. It was Peter who bragged that he would follow Christ even to death. However, not recognizing the weakness of his human nature, Peter denied Christ three times, as Jesus said he would. Yet Jesus told Peter, "I have prayed for thee, that thy faith fail not: and when thou art converted, strengthen thy brethren" (v. 32).

Jesus's prayer for Peter was answered. He preached a powerful sermon on the Day of Pentecost, and about three thousand souls were saved. He connected so deeply with His Lord that people were healed when his shadow fell on them (Acts 5:15). And his epistles in the New Testament (1 Peter and 2 Peter) are filled with insights of his intimate relationship with Christ.

5. In Luke chapter 23, when Jesus was hanging on the cross, a thief that was crucified beside Him appealed to Him for mercy. This condemned man had heard Christ declare of those who crucified Him, "Father, forgive them; for they know not what they do" (v. 34). He asked Jesus, "Lord, remember me when thou comest into thy kingdom." Jesus responded, "Verily I say unto thee, today shalt thou be with me in

paradise" (vv. 42–43). What a powerful revelation of the forgiving heart of God.

RECEIVING PERSONAL FORGIVENESS

In order to help us grasp the magnitude of God's forgiveness for our own needy hearts, Dr. Tom Woodward offers this analogy.[7] When we first seek forgiveness for our sin, we are ushered into the courtroom of God. There we discover that our court-appointed advocate is none other than Jesus Christ. He presents us to the Father and points to His sacrifice for our sins. We are justified on that basis. It is just as if we'd never sinned.

> **OUR COURT-APPOINTED ADVOCATE IS NONE OTHER THAN JESUS CHRIST.**

The Scriptures declare that when we are born again, there is no more condemnation for the believer (Rom. 8:1). We are also assured of ongoing forgiveness:

> My little children, these things I write to you, so that you may not sin. And if anyone sins, we have an Advocate with the Father, Jesus Christ the righteous. And He Himself is the propitiation for our sins, and not for ours only but also for the whole world....I write to you, little children, because your sins are forgiven you for His name's sake.
>
> —1 JOHN 2:1–2, 12, NKJV

The apostle John here exhorts the believer not to sin willfully. But when we do sin, we are assured that we have an advocate in Jesus, who will forgive us.

After we are born again, we move from God's courtroom into God's "family room." There, we experience the inviting warmth of a hearth with a fire burning and a father sitting there, welcoming us into the family of God as forgiven children of God. And when we recognize subsequent sin in our lives, we do not have to return to the courtroom of God; we become children of God, and our salvation is a settled matter from that time onward.

As a child of God, we have been forgiven of our sins. Here in the family room, we ask God's forgiveness for subsequent sin so that we can maintain fellowship with the Father. In that way, we grow in our faith and overcome any barrier to enjoying intimate communion with Him.

Again, the apostle John explains this ongoing process of growing in grace:

> If we confess our sins, he is faithful and just to forgive us our sins, and to cleanse us from all unrighteousness. If we say that we have not sinned, we make him a liar, and his word is not in us.
>
> —1 John 1:9–10

It is important to recognize the distinction between our initial audience with a holy God in His courtroom and our daily audience with God in His family room. Here we come to commune with our Father and be continually washed from any unrighteousness.

Understanding this distinction between our initial forgiveness and subsequent daily cleansing from sin can be a great help as we determine to walk with God and live before the face of the Father. Faithfully confessing our sins as a part of His family will maintain our uninterrupted fellowship with Him.

AT HOME IN DIVINE FELLOWSHIP

To Dr. Woodward's insightful analogy, I would like to add one more "room" the believer will want to occupy in his or her relationship with the Father. Passing from the "courtroom" to the "family room" and beyond, we observe a most inviting room indeed—I call it the "sunroom." It is here that we may bask in the warmth of God's divine light and His peace.

The sunroom is a place of fellowship where we are learning to continually rest in His redemption. We can wait in His presence, commune with Him, and cultivate relationship there. The sunroom is a blessed reward for those who have settled the sin question in the courtroom and learned to confess their sins daily in the family room.

Mother Teresa could have been referring to this sunroom when she said, "We need to find God, and he cannot be found in noise and restlessness. God is the friend of silence. See how nature—trees, flowers, grass—grows in silence; see the stars, the moon and the sun, how they move in silence.... We need silence to be able to touch souls."[8]

> **GOD IS A FRIEND OF SILENCE.**
> —MOTHER TERESA

In this divine sunroom, we enjoy what the psalmist called "the pleasures at His right hand forever." (See Psalm 16:11.) Walking in continual forgiveness gives us a chance to realize this promise of resting in His redemption. It is this place of intimate communion with the Father that equips us to become more useful for our purpose in life.

Integrity of faith

Of course, we must never take our personal forgiveness for granted. God forgives all sin, but He expects us to receive

His grace to keep from doing the same stupid, sinful things over and over again. Sin is contrary to God's plan for our lives and counterproductive to His good will for us. He desires for us to develop integrity of faith that consistently turns from sin to do the will of the Father.

WE HAVE BEEN INVITED BY A HOLY GOD JUST TO HANG OUT WITH HIM.

Jesus made this quite clear in His lesson about abiding in Him (John 15). He said He is the vine and we are the branches. Like a limb resting effortlessly as an outgrowth of a tree that produces fruit, so are we to rest in God's presence. We speak of friends just hanging out together. Without any sense of irreverence, we can say that we have been invited by a holy God just to hang out with Him. Jesus also said that He and the Father desire to live in us and we in Him:

> If a person [really] loves Me, he will keep My word [obey my teaching]; and My Father will love him, and We will come to him and make Our home (abode, special dwelling place) with him.
>
> —JOHN 14:23, AMP

> I am praying not only for these disciples but also for all who will ever believe in me through their message. I pray that they will all be one, just as you and I are one—as you are in me, Father, and I am in you. And may they be in us so that the world will believe you sent me.
>
> —JOHN 17:20–21, NLT

Do you see the mystery of romance with God Himself that the Scriptures offer to everyone who believes in Christ—to be *in* God the Father and *in* Christ the Son, and they *in* us? At home in God—incredible! Resting in that love relationship with God, who is love, is the ultimate love story fulfilled; it is available for every heart yearning for true contentment.

THE FAMILY OF GOD

As Christians, when we realize the glorious presence of Christ in our hearts, we are filled with an anointed dance of joy. His presence fills us with delight in doing His will. He imparts spiritual wisdom and understanding that open our mind to His eternal purpose.

As you cultivate that relationship, you will walk in heart satisfaction and know the contentment of fulfilling your divine destiny. Resting in His redemption brings an essence of freedom from sin and a capacity to explore intimacy with God without limits. Finding divine fulfillment in your relationship with God will lead you into right relationship with other Christians as well. You will begin to understand His divine purpose for His body in the earth, the church:

> The mystery of which was hidden for ages and generations [from angels and men], but is now revealed to His holy people (the saints), to whom God was pleased to make known how great for the Gentiles are the riches of the glory of this mystery, which is Christ within and among you, the Hope of [realizing the] glory.
> —COLOSSIANS 1:26–27, AMP

When Christ established His church in the earth, He did not intend for it to be a political or social organization. Neither did He design it to be a loosely joined religious affiliation. The apostle Paul uses the analogy of the human body to describe the church, with Christ being the head of the body and every believer one of the "members in particular" (1 Cor. 12:27).

In that inextricable union with God, we are connected with other believers in such a way that we cannot function effectively without their part. As we worship and pray together, receive the preached Word of God, and the sacraments of baptism, communion, and other biblical practices, we become the expression of Christ in the earth. In caring for one another's needs, we express the love that fulfills the law of Christ. That is the beauty of being a part of the body of Christ. It is God's provision for reaching our ultimate potential in Him.

REDEMPTION: PAST, PRESENT, AND FUTURE

> Through the redemption, God undertakes to deal with a man's past, and He does it in two ways: by forgiving him, and by making the past a wonderful culture for the future.
>
> —OSWALD CHAMBERS[9]

It is no wonder that even the angels desire to understand this divine mystery of our redemption (1 Pet. 1:12). This supernatural salvation works to redeem us so completely that it restores every part of our lives to God's purpose: our past, present, and future.

For our *past*, Christ died on the cross to provide salvation from the ravages of sin. When we accepted His sacrifice for our sin, we became new creatures in Christ Jesus (2 Cor. 5:17). Though we cannot change our past, when we submit our lives to His lordship, He can make our worst situation work for our good according to His purpose (Rom. 8:28).

In the *present*, as we learn to live with Him in the "family room," we receive ongoing cleansing through daily confession.

As our hearts are filled with the exhilaration of His forgiveness, we will want to hang out with Him in the "sunroom," where we enjoy fellowship in His light (1 John 1:7). His love fills us more and more as we learn to rest in His redemption in the present.

WHEN CHRIST ESTAB-LISHED HIS CHURCH IN THE EARTH, HE DID NOT INTEND FOR IT TO BE A POLITICAL OR SOCIAL ORGA-NIZATION.

In our *future* salvation, God will fulfill His promises of eternal bliss, of making us completely free from our sinful nature. No more will we suffer the mortality of our human bodies. And the eternal Sabbath rest of God will be ours forever, without end.

The Scriptures teach that as we wait before God, beholding His glory (2 Cor. 3:18), we receive the power of God's grace to change us and continually make us more like Him. In that divine mystery of personal intimacy with God, our past, present, and future redemption are sanctified to God's loving purposes. As we learn to receive His love, we will reflect His peace, His joy, and His divine glory in our lives.

PERSONAL MEDITATION

CHAPTER 4

What does forgiveness mean?

_____

_____

Can we ever comprehend how amazing "amazing grace" is?

_____

_____

Are we all sinners?

_____

_____

Does Christ accept us as sinners and totally forgive *all* our sins or just part of them?

_____

_____

What are the different rooms of forgiveness (redemption)?

_____

_____

After receiving God's redemption in His "divine courtroom," are we still held accountable for our actions in the family room? As we rest in His redemption, is this accountability increased? Do we sometimes still fail?

_____

_____

Can we walk in divine fellowship with God if we do not feel totally forgiven?

_____

_____

Does redemption have a past, a present, and a future?

_____

_____

PART 3

THE BIBLICAL BASIS FOR TOTAL FORGIVENESS IS RESTING IN HIS REDEMPTION

When we are bitter, we delude ourselves into thinking that those who hurt us are more likely to be punished as long as we are set on revenge.... This is a lie—the devil's lie.... We only hurt ourselves when we dwell on what has happened to us.... Most of all, we grieve the Holy Spirit of God, and this is why we lose our sense of peace.

—R. T. KENDALL[1]

Repose for the Redeemed

Of all the things I can know about God,
I have discovered that only a few are necessary.
He is good.
He is holy.
He is faithful.
He is sovereign.
All other truths hinge upon and stem from these four
    virtues.
Though no man can fully know God, it remains man's
    duty to know Him
To the degree He has revealed Himself to us.
So, whenever the circumstances of this life perplex or
    elude me,
I remind myself of this one simple truth.
The secret things belong to the Lord our God,
But the things revealed belong to us and to our children.
Therefore, I will stand firm on that which I have come to
    see and understand.
For while I cannot know all things,
I can hold fast to the One who does,
Knowing He works all things together for my good,
Because I love Him and am called according to His
    purpose.
I know of no greater rest than this,
That He who began a good work in me will bring it to
    completion.
So in the final analysis, it matters not upon the man
Who wills, or wants, or desires anything at all,
But upon God, who is faithful to do all things to His glory.
Therefore, because of what He is, I will praise His name
    forever and ever.
Amen.

—Jill MacGregor
(Used by Permission)

5

FORGIVING OTHERS

ORRIE TEN BOOM (1892–1983) was living with her older sister and her father in Haarlem when Holland surrendered to the Nazis. She was forty-eight, unmarried, and worked as a watchmaker with her father in the family jewelry store. Corrie's involvement with the Dutch underground began with her acts of kindness in giving temporary shelter to her Jewish neighbors who were being driven out of their homes.

She found places for them to stay in the Dutch countryside. Soon her home developed into the center of an underground ring that reached throughout Holland. Then an informant came to her home, posing as a family in need. Later that day her home was raided, and Corrie and her family were arrested. Corrie's father died from illness in prison within ten days of his capture.

Betsie, Corrie's sister, never strong in health, died in the Ravensbruck death camp in December of 1944. Some of her last words to her sister were: "Corrie, we must tell them that there is no pit so deep that God's love is not deeper still."

Due to a clerical error, Corrie was released from that camp one week before all other women her age were killed. Soon after her release, she began traveling and sharing the powerful message of forgiveness. She told the story of her family and the powerful lessons she and Betsie had learned in the concentration camp regarding forgiveness of her enemies.

> "WE MUST TELL THEM THAT THERE IS NO PIT SO DEEP THAT GOD'S LOVE IS NOT DEEPER STILL."
>
> —BETSIE TEN BOOM

It was never easy for Corrie; she did not have the strength of faith of her sister. Betsie encouraged Corrie to let go of her bitterness and receive the grace of God to love her enemies. After the war, Corrie was sharing with large audiences how forgiveness had become a reality in her life. She recalled a powerful incident that tested that reality:

It was at a church service in Munich that I saw him, the former S.S. man who had stood guard at the shower room door at Ravensbruck. And suddenly it was all there—the roomful of mocking men, the heaps of clothing....He came up to me as the church was emptying, beaming and bowing. "How grateful I am for your message...to think that He has washed my sins away!" His hand was thrust out to shake mine...I tried to smile, I struggled to raise my hand. I felt nothing, not the slightest spark of warmth or charity. And so again I breathed a silent prayer. "Jesus, I cannot forgive him. Give me Your forgiveness." As I took his hand, the most incredible thing happened. From my shoulder along my arm and through my hand a current seemed to pass from me to him, while into my heart sprang a love for this stranger that almost overwhelmed me.[1]

RECEIVING GRACE TO FORGIVE
YOUR ENEMIES

It is rare that you meet an individual who has not been hurt by another human being through betrayal, abuse, or some form of injustice. From our childhood, we sense the unfairness of treatment we receive from others, whether family, teachers, friends, employers, or a significant other.

When we suffer injustice, we must learn to rest in the peace of God's redemption and trust in His promises as the psalmist did:

> I will wait for You, O You his Strength; for God is my defense....I will sing of Your power; yes, I will sing aloud of Your mercy in the morning; for You have been my defense and refuge in the day of my trouble.
> —PSALM 59:9, 16, NKJV

Mean-spirited retaliation is not an option when we suffer an injustice done to us. Rather, we need to focus our minds on God and ask for the grace to love our enemies, as His Word commands us to do:

> You have heard the law that says, "Love your neighbor" and hate your enemy. But I say, love your enemies! Pray for those who persecute you! In that way, you will be acting as true children of your Father in heaven.
> —MATTHEW 5:43–45, NLT

When we call on the Lord and thank Him daily for helping us to live free from the sins of bitterness, anger, wrath, and revenge, He will give us grace to forgive our enemies.

When we are wounded and perplexed by injustice, even those administered by friends and family, it is imperative that we maintain our inner focus on our love relationship with our Lord. If we have learned that the priority of life as God intended it is to live in the mystery of divine romance, nothing must be allowed to separate us from our Beloved.

"Don't lose your anointing."

When my friend R. T. Kendall leaves my home at the end of a visit, he always says to me, "Don't lose your anointing." I am grateful for the reminder. The *anointing*, that tangible presence of the glory of Christ in me, must be treasured and guarded continually.

> MEAN-SPIRITED RETALIATION IS NOT AN OPTION WHEN WE SUFFER AN INJUSTICE DONE TO US.

I must not allow anger, resentment, unforgiveness, or any other sin to quench the anointing of the Holy Spirit. It is imperative that I determine to forgive others so that I don't grieve the Holy Spirit (Eph. 4:30). When I suffer injustice at the hands of another person, I need to pray for a conciliatory attitude; only then will I receive grace to bless my offender.

Regardless of your station in life, you should expect people to treat you justly. If they do not, you may confront them kindly and attempt to bring peace to the situation. If they are not willing to resolve the situation and there is just cause, you may need to allow the legal system to intervene.

For example, situations of child abuse or spousal abuse often need professional intervention for reasons of safety. Yet even in such challenging times, it is imperative that you pray for your enemies and receive grace from God to love them.

That is the secret to really being at peace in situations

where people try to take advantage of you. The psalmist knew how to seek God's grace for these trying situations:

> Fret not yourself because of evildoers, neither be envious against those who work unrighteousness (that which is not upright or in right standing with God). For they shall soon be cut down like the grass, and wither as the green herb. Trust (lean on, rely on, and be confident) in the Lord and do good; so shall you dwell in the land and feed surely on His faithfulness, and truly you shall be fed. Delight yourself also in the Lord, and He will give you the desires and secret petitions of your heart. Commit your way to the Lord [roll and repose each care of your load on Him]; trust (lean on, rely on, and be confident) also in Him and He will bring it to pass. And He will make your uprightness and right standing with God go forth as the light, and your justice and right as [the shining sun of] the noonday. Be still and rest in the Lord; wait for Him and patiently lean yourself upon Him....Cease from anger and forsake wrath; fret not yourself—it tends only to evildoing.... The meek [in the end] shall inherit the earth and shall delight themselves in the abundance of peace.
>
> —PSALM 37:1–7, 8, 11, AMP

BECOME AN INTERCESSOR—NOT AN ACCUSER

When a colleague and I suffered great financial loss through unjust trickery, my colleague became miserable because of the anger he harbored against those who had wronged us in a legitimate business transaction. In order for me to escape the same fateful reaction, I knew it was vitally important that I forgive these people. I am humbled and deeply grateful for the power of God's redemption to keep me resting in His redemption in that unfortunate situation.

In our own strength, we cannot maintain the right attitude when we are facing injustice or other difficult situations. We automatically become *accusers* of those who have wronged us unless we make a conscious decision to become an *intercessor*. To intercede in prayer for those who have harmed us, to forgive injustice, and to love our enemies require an intimate relationship with the God of love. His forgiving heart will flow into ours as we determine to rest in His grace and redemption.

> **THE RICHES WE HAVE IN GOD, WHICH CANNOT BE LOST, DO NOT COMPARE TO ANYTHING OF EARTHLY VALUE.**

Apart from our Redeemer, we are designated for a hellish existence. Our souls will be filled with strife and ill-at-ease feelings as we face life's challenges. The apostle John desired believers to have healthy souls and to receive the blessings of God:

> Beloved, I wish above all things that thou mayest prosper and be in health, even as thy soul prospereth.
> —3 JOHN 2

Our souls prosper when we cultivate the mystery of divine romance with our Redeemer. When we wait on Him, He gives us peace of mind that passes understanding. He establishes us in healthy emotional responses to face the most difficult situations of life.

The life that enjoys God eclipses anything else we might have in this life. All that we value here is temporal; it is our relationship with God that is eternal. The riches we have in

God, which cannot be lost, are infinitely greater than any-thing of earthly value. I love the extravagance of the gospel:

> He who did not withhold or spare [even] His own Son
> but gave Him up for us all, will He not also with Him
> freely and graciously give us all [other] things?
> —ROMANS 8:32, AMP

It is hard to imagine such a reckless love of our Creator-Redeemer, who created everything to give to us. He redeemed us to Himself so we could abandon ourselves to His love. As we experience such extravagant love, it provokes our hearts to reckless appreciation for our God; it becomes our highest priority to enjoy God and glorify Him.

Enjoying God and resting in His redemption are eternal gifts that alone can satisfy the human spirit. We are made for Him and are destined to glorify Him in all we do. That involves forgiving others when we suffer injustice at their hands.

A New Testament mandate

Christ's atonement is not only the remedy for our per-sonal sin. It is also the remedy for our inability to forgive those who sin against us. His supernatural grace empowers us to forgive the one who hurt us most deeply. As we com-mune with Him, we are filled with His grace. Then we are able to choose to forgive those who have sinned against us.

Do you remember what Christ spoke from the cross? He cried out, "Father, forgive them; for they know not what they do" (Luke 23:34). It is humanly impossible to under-stand the great love Jesus expressed toward His murderers in that prayer. Yet when Christ truly dwells within you, you can expect His love in your heart to respond to your worst enemies in that same way.

Jesus taught us to pray, "Forgive us our debts, as we forgive our debtors" (Matt. 6:12). And He taught that it is imperative to forgive our enemies if we are to have fellowship with God: "For if ye forgive men their trespasses, your heavenly Father will also forgive you: but if ye forgive not men their trespasses, neither will your Father forgive your trespasses" (Matt. 6:14–15). It is His divine love alone that will empower you to forgive those who have hurt you the most deeply.

Unforgiveness hurts you.

God had you in mind when He commanded you to forgive. It is a known scientific fact that resentment, bitterness, and unforgiveness harbored in the mind and heart will cause not only emotional distress but also physical disease as well. Jesus had your well-being in mind when He made it a divine requirement to walk in forgiveness toward others. He wants nothing to hinder you from living in intimate fellowship with Him. He wants your soul to prosper. He is interested in your peace and joy, which are not possible without walking in total forgiveness.

Unforgiveness works more destruction in your own soul than it does harm to your enemy. That is because unforgiveness breaks your fellowship with the Lord and prevents your receiving the forgiveness you need for peace with God. R. T. Kendall, in his powerful book *Total Forgiveness*, explains that when you choose to release your enemies from your unforgiveness, you are the one who will be set free:

> When everything in you wants to hold a grudge, point a finger, and remember the pain, God wants you to

lay it all aside. You can avoid spiritual quicksand and experience the incredible freedom found in total forgiveness.[2]

Jesus asked the searching question, "For if ye love them which love you, what thank have ye? for sinners also love those that love them" (Luke 6:32). Jesus gave this mandate filled with promise: "But love ye your enemies, and do good, and lend, hoping for nothing again; and your reward shall be great, and ye shall be the children of the Highest: for he is kind unto the unthankful and to the evil. Be ye therefore merciful, as your Father also is merciful" (Luke 6:35–36).

> **JESUS HAD YOUR WELL-BEING IN MIND WHEN HE MADE IT A DIVINE REQUIREMENT TO WALK IN FORGIVENESS TOWARD OTHERS.**

In *Pilgrim's Progress*, John Bunyan's classic analogy of the Christian life, Christian experienced release from a heavy load when he arrived on his journey to see the Celestial City. He was released from the burden of the world around him. Forgiveness of others brings a freedom very much like the lifting of a heavy load off our back. In forgiving our enemies, we are freed from carrying the harmful emotional load of retaliation, bitterness, and anger that threatens to destroy our souls.

FORGIVING THE WORST

Chuck Colson, author of *How Now Shall We Live?*,[3] discusses the options we have when we need to forgive another person. He asks the reader to consider how he or she would respond to a person who committed a heinous crime, such as molesting and killing their child. He suggests three possible reactions:

1. They could seek revenge and kill the perpetrator.

2. They could seek justice through the judicial system.

3. They could seek out the person, invite him into their home, forgive him, and offer him an inheritance in their estate.

What caring human being could naturally offer forgiveness to a criminal who killed their child? The natural reaction would be to kill him in revenge. A restrained response would be to seek legal justice for the crime committed. But receiving divine grace to forgive is the grace of God filling a heart that is truly resting in His redemption.

Colson cites this horrendous example of tragic injustice to show the magnitude of what Christ did for every sinner when He died on Calvary for our sin. He came to the earth to seek and to save men and women who sinned against God and against their neighbors. Set in this tragic human scenario, we can recognize how impossible is our task to forgive our enemies as God forgave us. We understand that forgiveness is truly a divine grace.

God's great, loving heart forgave every heinous act committed by mankind against Him. He offers to give sinners who repent an inheritance in His kingdom of love. Such grace is unfathomable, divine, and entirely supernatural. As the Scriptures declare, "Ye know the grace of our Lord Jesus Christ, that, though he was rich, yet for your sakes he became poor, that ye through his poverty might be rich" (2 Cor. 8:9).

God's great, loving heart forgave every heinous act committed by mankind against Him. He offers to give sinners who repent an inheritance in His kingdom of love. Such grace is unfathomable, divine, and entirely supernatural. As the Scriptures declare, "Ye know the grace of our Lord Jesus Christ, that, though he was rich, yet for your sakes he became poor, that ye through his poverty might be rich" (2 Cor. 8:9).

One of the greatest reasons we must determine to press into the rest of God (Heb. 4) is that we do not have the power in ourselves to forgive our enemies. While there is nothing in human nature that can conquer bitterness, resentment, or the desire for revenge, Jesus's command to love our enemies remains:

> GOD'S GREAT, LOVING HEART FORGAVE EVERY HEINOUS ACT COMMITTED BY MANKIND AGAINST HIM.

> But I say unto you which hear, Love your enemies, do good to them which hate you, bless them that curse you, and pray for them which despitefully use you....Love ye your enemies, and do good, and lend, hoping for nothing again; and your reward shall be great, and ye shall be the children of the Highest.
>
> —LUKE 6:27–28, 35

WHAT FORGIVENESS IS NOT

In order to be able to forgive effectively, it is important to understand what forgiveness is *not*. R. T. Kendall explains that forgiveness is not a *feeling*; it is a *choice* you make. In humble dependence on the supernatural grace of God, you choose to allow His divine love to flow through you toward your enemy. Having said that, to remove confusion that hinders us from forgiving, we also need to know what forgiveness is *not*. It is not:

1. Approving what they did

2. Excusing what they did

3. Justifying what they did

4. Pardoning what they did—for example, a criminal must pay his debt to society

5. Reconciliation—this requires the participation of two people

6. Denying what they did

7. Blindness to what happened

8. Forgetting what they did

9. Refusing to take the wrong seriously

10. Pretending we are not hurt[4]

God never approves, excuses, or justifies sin; He recognizes it for what it is and then chooses to forgive, based on His love through the atonement of Christ.

True forgiveness means being aware of the wrong and yet choosing to keep no record of it, refusing to punish, and relinquishing all bitterness and resentment toward your enemy—by the grace of God. When you make that choice, the Holy Spirit empowers you to truly forgive, and then He floods your soul with His peace and joy.

Forgiveness is a divine inner heart condition that responds to your enemy in mercy and gentleness.[5] It was the Holy Spirit's grace in Corrie ten Boom's heart that made it possible for her to choose to forgive the Ravensbruck guard.

RECEIVING GOD'S GRACE TO FORGIVE BRINGS YOUR SOUL INTO THE SUPER- NATURAL REST OF HIS LOVE.

When it seems impossible to your human mind that you would be able to forgive a deep hurt inflicted on you by another, let your faith in God's love help you appropriate this wonderful promise of God:

> But He said to me, My grace (My favor and loving- kindness and mercy) is enough for you [sufficient against any danger and enables you to bear the trouble manfully]; for My strength and power are made perfect (fulfilled and completed) and show themselves most effective in [your] weakness. Therefore, I will all the more gladly glory in my weaknesses and infirmities, that the strength and power of Christ (the Messiah) may rest (yes, may pitch a tent over and dwell) upon me!
>
> So for the sake of Christ, I am well pleased and take pleasure in infirmities, insults, hardships, persecu- tions, perplexities and distresses; for when I am weak [in human strength], then am I [truly] strong (able, powerful in divine strength).
>
> —2 CORINTHIANS 12: 9–10, AMP

The Holy Spirit revealed to the apostle Paul the supernatural power of God's grace for every kind of difficulty and distress. In your weakness, when you are tempted to harbor unforgiveness, His divine strength will help you to forgive. Receiving God's grace to forgive brings your soul into the supernatural rest of His love. In that place, the love of God will begin to supernaturally change your negative feelings toward those who have wronged you.

How to Know When You Have Totally Forgiven

The ultimate proof of total forgiveness takes place when we sincerely petition the Father to let those who have hurt us off the hook—even if they have hurt not only us, but also those close to us.

—R. T. Kendall[6]

You may wonder how to know if you have totally forgiven the one who betrayed you and altered your entire life through their unloving actions or words. R. T. Kendall writes that we will know when we have totally forgiven our enemies when we:

1. Don't tell others what they did to us

2. Don't let them fear us

3. Don't try to make them feel guilty

4. Let them save face

5. Protect them from their greatest fear

6. Make forgiveness a lifelong commitment

7. Pray for them to be blessed[7]

Each of these propositions is important to understand and practice. For example, it is not possible to assume we have totally forgiven just because we did it one time. According to Kendall, we must make forgiving others a "life sentence." We need to continually guard our hearts against the devil, who will look for ways to stir bitterness and resentment in our souls against others.[8]

> **FORGIVENESS IS NOT A *FEELING*; IT IS A *CHOICE* YOU MAKE.**
>
> —R. T. KENDALL

PERSONAL MEDITATION

CHAPTER 5

Do we have the power of forgiveness that Corrie ten Boom displayed when she totally forgave the people who persecuted her and killed her sister?

Can we forgive without receiving God's grace?

Does the Christian life need a continual source of anointing? Do we need to continually say to one another, "Don't lose your anointing"?

Which is more valid for a true Christian: becoming an intercessor or an accuser?

The person who hasn't forgiven himself is an unhappy
person—and is usually unable to forgive others.
—R. T. Kendall[1]

The very thing that haunts you most could turn out to
be the best thing that ever happened to you.
—R. T. Kendall[2]

6

FREEDOM FROM CONDEMNATION

THE FORGIVENESS OF our sins is the doorway to experiencing a relationship with God as our Father and Jesus Christ as our Savior. Zacharias, the father of John the Baptist, declared prophetically over his baby son:

> And thou, child, shalt be called the prophet of the Highest: for thou shalt go before the face of the Lord to prepare his ways; to give knowledge of salvation unto his people by the remission of their sins, through the tender mercy of our God; whereby the dayspring from on high hath visited us…to guide our feet into the way of peace.
> —LUKE 2:76–78, 79

We come to know God by the forgiveness of our sins through His tender mercy toward us. As I mentioned, receiving God's forgiveness is the doorway to knowing and walking with God. To know absolutely that my own sins are forgiven, to be convinced of that blessed reality, brings peace and the joy of salvation to my heart. It is God's part to forgive our repentant souls. It is our part to embrace God's pardon for our sins—every single one of them.

There will be a struggle at times to live above feelings of condemnation because of unbelief and doubt in our hearts.

We will be tempted to take back the shame and guilt in our minds that God has forgiven and forgotten. Though it is foolish of us to deny God's loving forgiveness, feelings of condemnation present a common battle that we all face at times.

As John Newton expressed in his famous hymn "Amazing Grace," we will find it hard to believe that God would "save a wretch like me." But we must receive the grace of God to believe it in order to enter into His peace and joy that He wants to give. The apostle Paul concluded his explanation of our struggle to be free from condemnation in our lives with this powerful declaration filled with hope:

> O wretched man that I am! who shall deliver me from the body of this death? I thank God through Jesus Christ our Lord.... There is therefore now no condemnation to them which are in Christ Jesus, who walk not after the flesh, but after the Spirit.
>
> —ROMANS 7:24–25; 8:1

If the apostle Peter had not been able to receive the grace of Christ's forgiveness for his personal denial of his Savior, his life would have been ruined. That devastating experience of denying his Lord and perceiving his own cowardice caused Peter to go out and weep bitterly (Matt. 26:75). He could not change what he had done.

There was only one way for Peter to move forward: he had to let go of the past and find the grace to accept Christ's total forgiveness. Otherwise, Jesus's prayer for him would not have been answered: "I have prayed for thee, that thy faith fail not: and when thou art converted, strengthen thy brethren" (Luke 22:32). Thankfully, Jesus's prayers will always be answered.

Did you know that Christ prays for you? Awesome as that

may seem, the Scriptures teach that Christ is now at the right hand of God making intercession for you (Rom. 8:34). In that same passage, the apostle Paul makes this bold declaration: "If God be for us, who can be against us?" (Rom. 8:31). The magnitude of these comforting truths teaches us that we can accept God's forgiveness for every sin we have committed or may yet commit.

DID YOU KNOW THAT CHRIST PRAYS FOR YOU?

It may be that you are your own worst enemy when it comes to condemning yourself. If that is the case, you need to receive by faith the anointed Word of God that no one can condemn you—not even you. Perhaps for some, this is the most difficult aspect of walking in divine forgiveness.

There is a current New Age teaching that says you can forgive yourself without receiving the power and grace of God to do so. That is a false, godless idea. The real guilt you feel for the sin you have committed cannot be forgiven by mental exercises or by doing subsequent good acts. It will not go away through denial. Only God can forgive sin. And unless you receive His divine forgiveness, accepting it by faith, your sense of guilt will remain.

"I Agree With God's Word"

It is a settled fact that all our freedom comes from Jesus Christ and His redemptive sacrifice on Calvary. There is no other source of liberty from the power of sin, guilt, and condemnation. It is our part to agree with His truth. We honor God when we say, "Thank You, God, that I know I am forgiven of that sin I committed, the one that haunts me.

Give me the faith to believe Your mercy toward me and Your promises concerning forgiveness for my sin."

> Who is a God like unto thee, that pardoneth iniquity...because he delighteth in mercy?...He will subdue our iniquities; and thou wilt cast all their sins into the depths of the sea.
>
> —MICAH 7:18–19

> Bless the LORD, O my soul, and forget not all his benefits.... For as the heaven is high above the earth, so great is his mercy toward them that fear him. As far as the east is from the west, so far hath he removed our transgressions from us.
>
> —PSALM 103:2, 11–12

> For they shall all know me, from the least of them unto the greatest of them, saith the LORD: for I will forgive their iniquity, and I will remember their sin no more.
>
> —JEREMIAH 31:34

Corrie ten Boom, survivor of the Holocaust prison camps, quaintly described God's merciful forgiveness of our sins this way: "When we confess our sins...God casts them into the deepest ocean, gone forever. And even though I cannot find a Scripture for it, I believe God then places a sign out there that says, NO FISHING ALLOWED."[3]

When you agree with the truth of God's Word, you can say boldly, "I know the blood of Jesus Christ cleanses me from all my sins. I know there is no condemnation for me in Christ (Rom. 8:1). I can look into the face of God and call Him my Father. He has forgiven me; I believe it, receive it, drink it in, and rest in the comfort of His loving heart toward me. I know He wants me to lift up my head and praise Him that He accepts me in the beloved family of God. I know He delights in me and welcomes me into His presence as a forgiven child of God."

Daily we must maintain our victory over guilt and condemnation by saying, "Today, Lord, I believe You took away all of my sins on the cross and You want me to rejoice in this cleansing and forgiveness that is mine." This disposition of daily declaring God's truth and resting in His redemption will become a fountain of gratitude that emanates into every area of our lives. When the fiery darts of the devil come after us, we must lift up the shield of faith and declare that we believe only what is written in the Word of God.

> IT TAKES A CONSCIOUS DECISION TO ACCEPT CHRIST'S REDEMPTION FROM THE CONDEMNA-TION AND GUILT THAT TORMENT YOU.

I resist the devil's fiery darts of condemnation and guilt when he tries to remind me of particularly haunting sins and when he tries to make me doubt the forgiveness God has given me. I declare the words of my Father in heaven that reveal His love for me and His mercy that has taken away all my sins: "Jesus, I receive Your words for me that You declared over the paralytic that day: 'Son, be of good cheer; thy sins be forgiven thee'" (Matt. 9:2).

It takes a conscious decision to accept Christ's redemptive power to erase the condemnation and guilt that torment you. Instead of agreeing with those negative thoughts, you embrace the grace of God's forgiving power in your life. As you wait on God in the "sunroom" of His presence, He will renew your mind and wash you of the unbelief that does not allow you to accept His forgiveness.

There in His presence, you can let go of your bitter, sinful experience and receive the comfort, love, and healing of Christ's redemption. There you can receive the wonderful reality of God's promise: "And truly our fellowship is with the Father, and with his Son Jesus Christ" (1 John 1:3). This freedom is one of the more powerful reasons for abandoning yourself to the mystery of divine romance with your Creator-Redeemer.

FAITH PERSEVERES

Faith will persevere in helping you believe the sovereign work of God's grace to forgive you—totally. It is that persevering personal conviction in God's grace that empowers you to receive His total forgiveness and be freed from condemnation. If you do not abandon yourself to the grace Jesus offers you, you simply do not believe in His lordship or His total forgiveness of your sin.

> YOU WILL RECEIVE GRACE TO LIVE ABOVE CONDEMNATION AS YOU DETERMINE TO REST IN THE COMPLETE REDEMPTION OF YOUR LORD.

That does not mean that it is always easy to persevere in faith against the condemning thoughts you carry about your past sin. You will need to spend time reading the Word of God and allowing the Holy Spirit to reveal to you His love and power. Without the anointing of the Word washing your mind with its divine truth, you will not be able to truly rest in His redemption, free from all condemnation.

God's Word teaches you how to persevere in faith against the old condemning thoughts that keep you in torment:

> Stand fast in the faith, quit you like men, be strong.
> —1 CORINTHIANS 16:13

> Stand fast therefore in the liberty wherewith Christ hath made us free, and be not entangled again with the yoke of bondage.
> —GALATIANS 5:1

> Stand therefore, having your loins girt about with truth, and having on the breastplate of righteousness; and your feet shod with the preparation of the gospel of peace; above all, taking the shield of faith, wherewith ye shall be able to quench all the fiery darts of the wicked. And take the helmet of salvation, and the sword of the Spirit, which is the word of God.
> —EPHESIANS 6:14–17

> Stand perfect and complete in all the will of God.
> —COLOSSIANS 4:12

You will receive grace to live above condemnation as you determine to rest in the complete redemption of your Lord. R. T. Kendall explains how the grace of God uses even your most "unforgivable" sin to work for your good according to His Word—"And we know that in all things God works for the good of those who love him, who have been called according to his purpose" (Rom. 8:28, NIV):

> Assuming you believe the Bible…if Romans 8:28 were unfolded before your eyes and you would accept

the literal truth of it, you would be set free....Why? Because Romans 8:28 was given to us precisely to help us never to feel guilty....

It refers to our entire past...all that happened to you before you were saved, but also to whatever has happened to you since you were saved....

Call to your mind your most difficult moment. Your most shameful. The hardest to understand. When you were at your worst. When the greatest injustice was thrust upon you. When you were involved in the most tragic accident—whether your fault or not. I could go on and on....

Romans 8:28 guarantees to every person who loves God and is among the called according to His purpose that anything and everything that was negative, wrong, or unfair that has happened to them will eventually turn out for *good*.[4]

As you choose to believe the Word of God and receive the grace you need to accept God's forgiveness for yourself, you will lose the fear of punishment by God; you will enter into peace and freedom from the bondage of personal guilt and condemnation.

When you are released from the paralysis of guilt for past failures, accepting God's total forgiveness will help you to love others more. Your physical and mental health will also improve as you rest in His redemption and enjoy the peace of God in your soul by placing your faith in Him.

Faith Enjoys the Grace of a Pure Heart

Jesus said, "Blessed are the pure in heart: for they shall see God" (Matt. 5:8). As you accept God's cleansing of your heart for every sin, His shed blood will purify your heart so that you will enjoy intimate relationship with Him; you will see God.

Jean Pierre de Caussade explains the value of a pure heart:

> A pure heart and perfect abandonment bring us all the treasures of grace....I, my Lord, ask for one thing only and have only a single prayer—give me a pure heart! How happy we are if our hearts are pure! Through the ardor of our faith we see God as he is....The pure heart could well say to every soul: "Look at me carefully. It is I who generates that love which chooses the better part and clings to it...I who imparts that excellent understanding which reveals the greatness of God and the merit of virtue. And it is also I who causes that passionate and holy yearning which keeps the soul resolute in virtue in the expectation of that enjoyment of God which will one day, more perfectly than now, be the delight of every faithful soul."[5]

FORGIVENESS THROUGH CONFESSION

Unforgiveness toward others and self-condemnation are huge barriers to enjoying the mystery of your romance with the Lord. To overcome these hindrances, you must be diligent—daily—to make the choice to receive God's forgiveness for your sin (in the "family room"). You must be willing to forgive others. And you must be determined to defeat the devil's accusations against you that keep you living under a load of condemnation (in the "sunroom"). Of course, all this wonderful freedom is

PERSONAL CONFESSION IS THE WAY TO EXPERIENCE GREAT CLEANSING AND RENEWAL.

because the "courtroom" is a settled issue in our salvation experience.

According to the Scriptures, personal confession is the way to experience great cleansing and renewal that allow you to rest in His redemption. The Scriptures declare: "If we confess our sins, he is faithful and just to forgive us our sins, and to cleanse us from all unrighteousness" (1 John 1:9). You dare not doubt the faithfulness of God to fulfill His promises in your life. He promises to forgive you and cleanse you from all unrighteousness when you simply confess your sins.

David Powlison, a leader of the Christian Counseling and Education Foundation (CCEF), offers this helpful advice for the success of your personal confession:

> I suggest that you pray out loud. It helps you to remember that you are talking with someone who is listening. You aren't just thinking things inside your head. Use this prayer to express the gravity of what happened. Use it to remind yourself out loud that God's mercies are deeper than what you did or failed to do...
>
> The beauty of the gospel is that our confession is always linked with God's promise of good. Guilt and regret make you miserable: unhappy, in dire need of mercy. Mercy is not something anyone deserves; it is something undeserved that someone else gives.[6]

When the Holy Spirit reminds you of an offense that is lodging in your heart against someone who hurt you, be quick to speak forgiveness over that person by name. When He convicts you of personal sin, quickly bow in a prayer of repentance and confession, asking God to cleanse you. As you practice walking diligently in total forgiveness, you will enjoy the wonderful peace of God and become established in a life of intimate fellowship with Christ. When doubt arises in your heart regarding God's loving, forgiving heart, declare His promises:

> But this I recall and therefore have I hope and expectation: it is because of the Lord's mercy and loving-kindnesses that we are not consumed, because His [tender] compassions fail not. They are new every morning; great and abundant is Your stability and faithfulness.
>
> —LAMENTATIONS 3:21–23, AMP

In summary, resting in His redemption is only possible as you choose, first of all, to accept God's forgiveness for your sin. Then you must determine to forgive others. Only by completely appropriating the supernatural grace of God for forgiveness can you live a life that is continually free from the misery of unforgiveness and condemnation. As you choose to place your faith in Christ alone, He will be faithful to let you enjoy the restful grace of His redemption, for which you were created.

PERSONAL MEDITATION

CHAPTER 6

Is it sometimes hard to live in freedom from condemnation?

_____

_____

Does God's Word promise that your sins will be forgotten when you ask for His cleansing?

_____

When you say, "I agree with God's Word and receive His forgiving grace," are you saying that you really *believe* the promise of God's Word that He has forgiven you? Are you consciously deciding to accept the reality of God's cleansing and forgiveness and to stop listening to the condemnation in your thoughts?

Can faith persevere in believing the sovereign work of God's grace to forgive you—totally?

Will the grace of God use even your most "unforgivable" sin to work for your good according to His Word? (See Romans 8:28.)

Will accepting the grace of God to free you from condemnation help you love others more?

PART 4

THE BIBLICAL BASIS FOR DIVINE CONTENTMENT IS RESTING IN HIS REDEMPTION

Contentment in every condition is a great art, a spiritual mystery. It is to be learned, and to be learned as a mystery....Contentment is a sweet, inward heart-thing. It is a work of the Spirit indoors.
—JEREMIAH BURROUGHS (1599–1646)[1]

I have learned how to be content (satisfied to the point where I am not disturbed or disquieted) in whatever state I am.

—PHILIPPIANS 4:11, AMP

Don't waste any sympathy on me. I am the happiest person living.

—FANNY CROSBY,
BLIND SINCE INFANCY[1]

7

DIVINE CONTENTMENT

BLINDED IN HER infancy, Frances Jane Crosby (1820–1915) was destined to become one of the greatest hymn writers in the history of the Christian church. Better known as the beloved Fanny Crosby, one of her most poignant lines of poetry reveals her intimate love relationship with Christ: "And I shall see Him face to face, and tell the story—saved by grace."[2]

Born in a one-story cottage, Fanny would never remember her father, for he died in her twelfth month. When Fanny was six weeks old, a viral infection affected her eyes. The family physician was away, and another country doctor was called in to treat her. He prescribed hot mustard poultices to be applied to her eyes, which destroyed her sight completely. It was later learned that the man was not qualified to practice medicine, but by then he had left town and was never heard of again.

What bitter tragedy altered the life of this innocent baby and, indeed, her entire family. Her wise mother set about immediately to prepare her daughter for a happy life, in spite of this great handicap. When she was but five years old, Fanny was taken to consult the best eye specialist in the country, Dr.

Valentine Mott. After the examination, the dreaded answer came: "Poor child, I am afraid you will never see again."

But Fanny did not think she was "poor." It was not the loss of sight that bothered her young heart. It was the thought that she would never be able to get an education like other boys and girls. Still, she maintained a sunny disposition in spite of the darkness in which she lived. At the age of eight, Fanny wrote her first recorded poetry:

> Oh, what a happy soul I am,
> Although I cannot see,
> I am resolved that in this world
> Contented I will be.
>
> How many blessings I enjoy
> That other people don't!
> To weep and sigh because I'm blind,
> I cannot and I won't![3]

Fanny's mother introduced her to the Bible at a young age, which became more familiar to her than any other book. It is said that as a child she could recite from memory the Pentateuch (Genesis through Deuteronomy), the Book of Ruth, many of the psalms, the Books of Proverbs and Song of Solomon, and much of the New Testament!

Fanny's knowledge of the Scriptures led her into her life-long friendship with God, who became the supreme source of her deep contentment. This divine friendship would later furnish the themes, inspiration, and words for her hundreds of beloved gospel hymns.

Near her fifteenth birthday came a happy announcement: Mother could send her to a new school, the Institution for the Blind in New York City. Fanny clapped her hands joyfully and cried, "O, thank God, He has answered my prayer, just as I knew He would."[4] She was to spend the next twenty-three years of her life there. For twelve years, she was a student; then she became a teacher of the institute for eleven years more. It was there that Fanny would meet her future husband.

From early childhood, this sightless girl felt the urge to write poetry. At the Institution for the Blind, her abilities began to assert themselves with renewed force. Her teachers did not encourage her efforts, but strangers did. William Cullen Bryant, renowned journalist, poet, and editor-in-chief of the *New York Evening Post* for half a century, visited the school one day. He gave Fanny much encouragement after

> TO WEEP AND SIGH BECAUSE I'M BLIND, I CANNOT AND I WON'T!
>
> —FANNY CROSBY

chancing to read some of her verses. She said afterward, "By those few words he did inestimable good to a young girl."[5]

Fanny's deepening friendship with God gave her the grace to keep her heart free from such sins as bitterness and self-pity. She gave no place to resentment because of her irreversible blindness, despite the criminal carelessness that had plunged her whole life into darkness. Instead, she let her heart be filled with joy and praises for her loving Savior.

Such contentment exuded from Fanny's life that it was obvious a supernatural grace was working there. Fanny once said, "Mother, if I had a choice, I would still choose to remain blind...for when I die; the first face I will ever see will be the face of my blessed Saviour."[6] She had discovered the mystery of romance with her wonderful Lord and was learning to rest in the comfort of His redemption.

During her lifetime, Fanny Crosby wrote over eight

thousand poems that were set to music, and over one million copies of her songs were printed. Fanny gave the Christian world such classic hymns as "All the Way My Savior Leads Me," "Blessed Assurance," "Close to Thee," "He Hideth My Soul," "I Am Thine O Lord," "My Savior First of All," "Near the Cross," and "Safe in the Arms of Jesus," to mention a few.

When still a young woman, Fanny Crosby achieved great notoriety as a guest of the US Congress. She wrote an original poem to include in her lecture to them. Before long, tears were glistening on the hearers' cheeks. That notable assembly to which she spoke included men like John Quincy Adams and Jefferson Davis.

Fanny spoke with conviction, as though she had seen the Savior face-to-face. As a result of this joyful witness, she began to make friends with the great political and religious leaders of her time, including presidents Martin Van Buren, William Henry Harrison, and James K. Polk. And she enjoyed a close friendship with President Grover Cleveland for more than half a century. Throughout her life, thousands of people, whether great or small, have found Fanny's message of a loving God a healing balm for their souls.

Fanny Crosby was happily married for forty-four years to a fellow blind teacher, Alexander Van Alstyne. He wrote the music of some of her hymn-poems. The couple had one child who was taken in death while yet a baby. Perhaps this incident helped inspire Fanny to write her beloved hymn, "Safe in the Arms of Jesus." Whatever its inspiration, it is considered by some to be her greatest hymn. It has offered comfort for decades to thousands of grief-stricken parents suffering a similar loss.

At age ninety, Fanny declared, "My love for the Holy Bible

and its sacred truth is stronger and more precious to me at ninety than at nineteen."[7] One of her famous sayings in life was, "Don't waste any sympathy on me. I am the happiest person living."[8] Such a life of contentment evoked admitted envy from "sighted" people who knew no such rest and delight in her Savior. Fanny Crosby had truly learned the blessed life found only in resting in His redemption.

Christian Contentment: A Rare Jewel

What was the secret to Fanny Crosby's long life of contentment that transcended her life's challenges? Why do so many Christians who suffer no such physical limitations find it difficult to lay hold of the happiness she relished during her long life? I believe it is because they have an ill-defined concept of true contentment and a misplaced focus on pursuing gratification in the temporal things of the world.

I have a friend who was unhappy in a place of employment. The job was not working out the way he had expected. Because he found no way to remedy the situation, he fell into a state of total despair. As a believer, he did not seek rest in the security of his redemption. Instead, he allowed his circumstances to govern his thoughts and emotions.

My friend ignored the true source of peace and joy found in our Lord. Instead, his focus was on what he was unable to achieve in his career because of his employment situation. As a result, he was trapped in his misery.

Missionary friends Ralph and Susan McIntosh come by occasionally to visit with us. Ralph shared what he calls the opposite of Christian contentment: *the agony of attainment.* What a great phrase to describe people like my friend who are totally focused on what they can achieve themselves—people who live in disappointment because they look to personal attainment as their source of happiness. In their frantic pursuit of happiness, they fail to focus on resting in the redemption of their Lord where they could enjoy His peace, joy, and divine contentment.

When Ralph and Susan pray, they sometimes hold out their arms and declare over a situation or a person, "Peace, be still; peace, be still." What an important declaration in our times of trial, whether in war or disasters, personal conflict or tragedy! Christ offers those who learn to abide in Him the jewel of contentment for the agony of attainment. We need to speak peace, in Jesus's name, into all of our situations and relationships that are in turmoil. In spite of circumstances, we can live in divine contentment.

> THE OPPO-
> SITE OF
> CHRISTIAN
> CONTENT-
> MENT IS *THE
> AGONY OF
> ATTAINMENT.*
>
> —RALPH
> MCINTOSH

No relationship is exempt from conflict, so it is good to pray "Peace, be still" with the authority given to us in Christ. Jesus told His disciples, "Peace I leave with you, my peace I give unto you: not as the world giveth....Let not your heart be troubled, neither let it be afraid" (John 14:27).

FREEDOM FROM FEAR

As I have mentioned, fear entered the human race when Adam and Eve disobeyed God's command. When they heard His voice in the garden, they ran to hide themselves from their Creator. Fear always rules where there is disobedience and conflict. Jesus came to redeem us from that natural fear and to offer us His divine peace.

Do you remember the incident when Jesus and the disciples were on a boat and a great storm arose? Jesus was sleeping, and the disciples, fearing the worst, began to panic. They called to Jesus for help. He awoke and rebuked the wind, saying to the sea, "Peace, be still" (Mark 4:39). In that moment, the wind ceased and there was a great calm. Jesus wants us to know that same peace and freedom from fear in our personal storms of life.

One of the great benefits of learning to rest in God's redemption is to enjoy His supernatural freedom from fear. The Scriptures teach that God is love and that love casts out fear (1 John 4:16–18). Until we have allowed the love of God to deliver us from our fears, contentment will elude us. As we turn to God in every fearful situation, we will learn to receive His peace, joy, and contentment.

"I Have Learned to Be Content"

The apostle Paul taught us that contentment is a character trait and quality of life that has to be learned:

> I have learned how to be content (satisfied to the point where I am not disturbed or disquieted) in whatever state I am.
> —Philippians 4:11, AMP

Jeremiah Burroughs, whom we earlier discussed, published a book of his sermons called *The Rare Jewel of Christian Contentment* based on this assertion of the apostle Paul. Burroughs reasons with believers concerning how to find contentment in every aspect of life.

Though he lived in a different century, the concepts Burroughs taught regarding the true source of Christian contentment are amazingly applicable in today's culture of discontentment. So basic are his teachings to the reality of human nature that they transcend time to speak to our twenty-first-century challenges.

Contentment, according to Burroughs, is *an art and a mystery* that must be learned. Especially for a sorrowing heart or one facing trouble, there is a great mystery involved in learning to be content. It is in embracing the grace of God that the mystery of contentment becomes a reality for the believer. Burroughs urges us to make the pursuit of that mystery our priority in this life in order to enjoy tranquility of soul in every circumstance.[9]

Defiance vs. contentment

According to Burroughs, contentment is a sweet, inward heart reality. It is not an outward cessation of activity or even a lack of stressful circumstances. It is an absence of fretting, anxiety, murmuring, or tumult in the heart even when facing life's distractions or consuming cares. Contentment is the opposite of despair and defiance; it is a quiet spirit that rests in God's grace and redemption.

Defiance, that disposition to resist and contend, is the determination to have our own way in life. It especially characterizes the behavior of children but is not absent from many adults. Defiance is reflected when someone covets goods or opportunities that they value. It involves pushing others away who do not acquiesce to their desires or serve their ends. There is no peace or rest in defiance, only contention, selfishness, and unrest.

A person who lives in defiance is a controlling person who demands life on their terms. They are miserable when circumstances or people impede their selfish demands. In a family, when a wife or mother is controlling (which some doctors consider pathological behavior), her family lives in turmoil rather than peace, in contention rather than Christian caring. A defiant, controlling person is driven by pride, insecurity, and fear. In short, defiance is the antithesis of resting in His redemption.

Defiance, that natural controlling selfishness, has no place in the heart of a believer. That is why Jesus taught His followers, "If any man will come after me, let him deny himself, and take up his cross, and follow me. For whosoever will save his life shall lose it: and whosoever will lose his life for my sake shall find it" (Matt. 16:24–25).

> CONTENTMENT
> IS A SWEET,
> INWARD
> HEART
> REALITY.
> —JEREMIAH
> BURROUGHS

Even as a Christian, you can only enjoy this rare jewel of contentment when you understand that all you need for life depends on your submission to the covenant that God has made with you in Christ. Though there is no certainty in worldly things, you can be secure in the everlasting covenant that makes you one with the Lord: "He that is joined unto the Lord is one spirit" (1 Cor. 6:17). The apostle John declared: "Beloved, now are we the sons of God" (1 John 3:2). He is a loving Father into whose hands we can commit our entire lives.

This covenant relationship with Christ is the source of all our contentment; it must become the focus of all our pursuits. There can be no contentment in this life without complete submission to Christ, taking pleasure in His will for our lives in every situation. Burroughs explains our happy submission to Christ in this manner:

> The soul before sought after this, and the other thing, but now faith the soul, I see really that it is not necessary that I should be rich, but it is necessary that I should make up my peace with God; it is not necessary that I should live a pleasurable life in this world, but it is absolutely necessary that I should have pardon of my sin; it is not necessary that I should have honour and preferment, but it is necessary that I should have God to be my portion and have my part in Jesus Christ...the other things are pretty fine things indeed, and I should be glad if God would give them to me, a fine habitation, and comings in, and clothes...I may have these, and yet perish forever, but the other is absolutely necessary.[10]

Learning Contentment

Burroughs refers to the "mystery of contentment" as a learned skill—an art—that rules in the soul, which is totally focused on resting in the loving redemption of God. He reminds us of the lesson Jesus taught Martha about the priorities of life.

Martha complained that her sister, Mary, was sitting at the feet of Jesus instead of helping her prepare a meal for Him. Jesus answered: "Martha, Martha, you are worried and troubled about many things. But one thing is needed, and Mary has chosen that good part, which will not be taken away from her" (Luke 10:42, NKJV). According to our Lord, the pursuit of intimate relationship and communion with Him is the one thing that is necessary to our contentment.

When you seek intimate communion with God, He becomes your contentment; you cannot be satisfied with any lesser activity. Even doing good things for Christ cannot substitute for the ultimate pleasure of sitting at His feet. And according to Jesus, the satisfaction of His presence will not be taken away from you.

While the mystery of contentment in life does not preclude sorrow or trouble, it offers a perspective for facing trouble without losing your peace and without being distracted from your focus on love Himself. The supernatural grace of contentment is strong enough to carry you through all situations in life.

Even if your worldly condition would be considered prosperous and extravagant, there is no true satisfaction to be found with the enjoyment of everything the world has to offer; the human heart can only be truly content in the mystery of divine romance—

> A PERSON WHO LIVES IN DEFIANCE IS A CONTROLLING PERSON WHO DEMANDS LIFE ON THEIR TERMS.
>
> —JEREMIAH BURROUGHS

continual communion with God. Let's remember once more the words of St. Augustine: "Thou hast formed us for Thyself, and our hearts are restless till they find rest in Thee."[11]

False sources of contentment

Even in seventeenth-century England, Burroughs argued that the world is infinitely deceived in thinking that contentment lies in acquiring more than we already have. He concludes that contentment is not always clothed with silk and purple and velvet; it is sometimes found in a homespun suit and in lowly circumstances.[12]

Burroughs calls the root of contentment the "evenness and proportion between our hearts and our circumstances."[13]

In other words, the degree of our contentment is reflected in the way our hearts respond to our outward conditions.

Do we depend on what we possess of worldly goods for our happiness? Are we relying on fame, political influence, human relationships, or other natural pleasures for our contentment? Burroughs contrasts the godly soul that has found true contentment with those who seek worldly happiness:

> The men of the world seek after wealth, and think if they had thus much they would be content....But a gracious heart says that if he had the quintessence of all the excellences of all the creatures in the world, it could not satisfy him; and yet this man can sing and be merry and joyful when he has only a crust of bread and a little water in the world....Great is the mystery of godliness....Godliness teaches us this mystery, not to be satisfied with all the world for our portion, and yet to be content with the meanest condition in which we are.[14]

As Christians, we have not always known how much more excellent and satisfying our relationship with God can be than anything we could hope to attain in this world. The fact is that we were made for God; there is nothing in this world that we can substitute for that innate desire to know Him. Nothing can replace the fulfillment found in bringing glory to Him in all we do.

THE MOST CONTENTED SOUL IN GOD WILL BE MOST DISSATISFIED WITH THE THINGS OF THE WORLD.

To that end, the most contented soul in God will be most dissatisfied with the things of the world. He or she will cry with the psalmist: "Whom have I in heaven but thee? and there is none upon earth that I desire beside thee" (Ps. 73:25). That is to say, we cannot find contentment apart from God Himself.

Even the blessings God gives to His children cannot substitute for the gift of God Himself, which is the mystery of divine romance that motivates our passion to enter more completely into the rest of His redemption. For example, God promises peace to His children. Yet even divine peace cannot satisfy the godly heart that longs for the *God* of that peace. He wants to enjoy the giver of all good gifts, not just the gifts themselves.[15]

The apostle Paul learned to be content in all circumstances because his heart was completely submitted to God. His life pursuit was to know God Himself and then to fulfill his high calling, in spite of the suffering that he might experience in this world.

In the classroom of contentment

The apostle Paul teaches practical ways to learn the art of being content. For example, he declared, "And whatsoever ye do in word or deed, do all in the name of the Lord Jesus, giving thanks to God and the Father by him" (Col. 3:17). In this context, Paul is instructing believers *how* to "seek those things which are above, where Christ sitteth on the right hand of God" (v. 1). He is teaching us how to bring glory to God in all we do.

Burroughs instructs believers to "labour to bring thy heart to quiet and contentment, by setting thy soul on work about the duties of your present condition."[16] How many of us have disdained the present situation we are in, using it merely as a stepping stone for loftier goals and personal pursuits? When we do that, we foster discontentment with our present circumstances instead of living every moment to bring glory to the Lord:

> So it is with many who think, If I were in such circumstances, then I should have contentment; and perhaps they get into those circumstances, and they are as far from contentment as before. Rather, the godly soul will learn the art of contentment when he allows the melting of his will and desires into God's will and desires.... It is said of believers that they are joined to the Lord, and are one spirit; that means, that whatever God's will is, I do not only see good reason to submit to it, but God's will is my will.[17]

This submissive attitude to God, which is the proper attitude of the believer, reflects the learned skill acquired for Christian contentment. The psalmist expressed his submission to God when he declared: "He shall choose our inheritance for us" (Ps. 47:4) and again, "The LORD will perfect that which concerneth me" (Ps. 138:8).

This trusting attitude shows the way to divine contentment, allowing God to reflect His will in our lives. That is in stark contrast to pursuing temporal goals to make my life condition more comfortable. Accepting God's inheritance means purging out my covetousness, lusts, and selfish desires. It is the reality of denying myself to follow Christ's pathway for my life. It is in knowing that God alone can perfect His plan in my life as I submit to His wisdom.

Fanny Crosby's ability to reflect a sunny disposition lay in the grace she received from her Savior to accept the "cross" of her blindness without bitterness or self-pity. As she submitted her heart to God, her spirit was free to "see" this mystery of divine contentment. She lived her life according to her inheritance, which was chosen by God, and she enjoyed intimate relationship with Him.

Did God allow her blindness as part of His mysterious will for her life? Yes. And He was there to comfort her in her affliction. He was able to make it work for her good, showing her the true source of contentment in life. By His grace, her affliction became like the wings of an eagle, causing her to soar to indescribable heights of achievement and notoriety. Fanny's friendship with God allowed her to transcend the darkness of her personal circumstances and enjoy the divine light of His presence during her long, productive, and inspiring life.

THE SWEETNESS OF GOD'S GIVING US GIFTS

Burroughs also describes contentment in God as the *mystery of enjoyment* that comes simply because we receive gifts from God: "Every good thing the people of God enjoy, they enjoy it in God's love, as a token of God's love, and coming from God's eternal love unto them, and this must needs be very sweet unto them."[18] In other words, just the fact that it is *God* who gives us a gift becomes a sweeter reality even than the gift itself.

This added dimension of contentment comes to those who recognize the hand of God giving to them because of His love for them. The apostle James wrote, "Every good gift and every perfect gift is from above, and cometh down from the Father of lights, with whom is no variableness, neither shadow of turning" (James 1:17). Burroughs concludes:

> This is a mystery to the wicked: I have what I have out of the love of God, and I have it sanctified to me by God, and I have it free of cost from God by the purchase of the blood of Jesus Christ, and I have it as a forerunner of those eternal mercies that are reserved for me; and in this my soul rejoyces [*sic*]. There is a secret dew of God's goodness and blessing upon him [who looks to God]...and by all this you may see the meaning of that Scripture, Prov. 16:8. *Better is a little with righteousness than great revenues without right.*[19]

The "secret dew" is a mystery of enjoyment that reflects the presence of God in a life. Whether in prosperity or affliction, the submissive heart learns that "all the paths of the LORD are mercy and truth unto such as keep his covenant and his testimonies" (Ps. 25:10). They understand that the mystery of contentment is not affected by circumstance, no matter how apparently good or bad it may seem. Instead, it is strengthened in every apparent goodness and blessing of God in their life.

I have mentioned the New Testament promise that "all things work together for good to them that love God, to them who are the called according to his purpose" (Rom. 8:28). This promise becomes a reality to those who dare to trust God with their whole life. It does not mean that all things are *good*. But God's love will transcend the evil and make it work for good for those who love Him and trust Him whole-heartedly. Burroughs contends:

> One drop of the sweetness of heaven is enough to take away all the sower [*sic*] and bitter of all the afflictions in the world.... There is no works that God hath made, the sun, moon, and stars and all the world wherein so

much of the glory of God doth appear, as in a man that lives quietly in the midst of adversity.[20]

This pursuit of divine contentment is what motivated New Testament saints who faced great persecution, even martyrdom, because they were followers of Christ. Paul and Silas were beaten and thrown into stocks in prison, yet they sang praises at midnight in spite of their pain and misery and uncertain future. Many were martyred for their faith, as Hebrews 11 attests, without renouncing their relationship with their loving Lord. This strength of grace, according to Burroughs, is also a fruit of contentment.

Contentment is reflected in a compound of the divine graces of faith, humility, love, patience, and wisdom. It embodies the respect that every creature owes the Creator. The contented soul will reveal this posture of worship in developing a personal life of prayer, devotion to the Word, and submission to the providence of God. These outward expressions of worship reflect the inward submission of a quieted heart, humbled in the fear of God and reveling in the mystery of divine romance.

This "jewel of contentment" is but a glimmer of what we will enjoy throughout eternity in the presence of our loving Lord. If we seek to worship Him here and to enter into the mystery of romance with Him, we can know days of heaven on earth, no matter what our outward circumstances.

OPPOSING CONTENTMENT: OUR MURMURING

A murmuring spirit opposes a contented heart that is in love with the Savior. Murmuring reveals much corruption in the soul, expressing intense discontentment with everything in life.

It must be cleansed before you can be healed and have the hope of experiencing the mystery of divine contentment. It is not the trouble you face or the vexation of others that makes you discontented; it is the "inflammation" of murmuring in your heart that makes you miserable.[21]

Have you considered the seriousness of your complaining, murmuring words against everything you find distasteful in life? "To murmur when we enjoy abundance of mercie [*sic*]," says Burroughs, "the greater and the more abundant the mercie is that we enjoy, the greater and the viler is the sin of murmuring."[22]

The Scriptures rank this sin as worthy of the judgment of God. Jude declares that when the Lord comes back with ten thousands of His saints, it will be to "execute judgment upon all, and to convince all that are ungodly among them of all their ungodly deeds…and of all their hard speeches which ungodly sinners have spoken against him. These are murmurers, complainers, walking after their own lusts; and their mouth speaketh great swelling words, having men's persons in admiration because of advantage" (Jude 15–16).

A MURMURING SPIRIT OPPOSES A CONTENTED HEART THAT IS IN LOVE WITH THE SAVIOR.

Murmuring and complaining reveal a defiant heart that the Bible calls ungodly. It is contrary to the contented heart filled with worship. Burroughs says, "How opposite is a murmuring discontented heart to a heart subdued to Jesus Christ as a King, and receiving him as a Lord to rule and dispose of [a man] as he pleases."[23]

The practical solution to entering into divine contentment

is to realize that murmuring is against the holiness, goodness, and mercy of God to you. The only way to enjoy the reality of contentment is to repent when you recognize in yourself this complaining spirit. Consider praying this prayer of repentance for your murmuring spirit:

> Oh how far have I been from this grace of contentment.... I have had a murmuring, a vexing, and fretting heart within me, every little cross hath put me out of temper and out of frame, O the boisterousness of my spirit! What a deal of evil doth God see...in the vexing and fretting of my heart, and murmuring and repining of my spirit?[24]

Then, after sincere repentance, it is your responsibility to give yourself to God in an everlasting covenant:

> The sight of the excellencie [*sic*] of Jesus Christ is to continue, and thy calling out of the creature, and thy casting of thy soul upon Christ as a King, still receive him day by day; and the subduing of thy heart, and the surrendering of thy self up to God in a way of covenant; now if this were but daily continued, there would be no space nor time for murmuring to work upon thy heart.[25]

This beautiful description of living a life of self-denial is the remedy for a murmuring, rebellious spirit. Left unchecked, the sin of murmuring will prevent you from finding the "rare jewel of Christian contentment."

Consequences of Discontentment

We have discussed how murmuring and discontentment hinder your relationship with God, with Christ, and with the Holy Spirit. As a child of God, you call Him Father, and you ask Him for your daily bread. As the bride of Christ, you are married to Him. Yet through murmuring, you dishonor Him like a spouse who goes whining around in discontentment.

> THE GREATER AND THE MORE ABUNDANT THE MERCIE IS THAT WE ENJOY, THE GREATER, AND THE VILER IS THE SIN OF MURMURING.
>
> —JEREMIAH BURROUGHS

And as a temple of the Holy Spirit, you are responsible to make Him feel welcome. This heavenly Comforter is responsible to convey all comforts from the Father and the Son to your heart. If you grieve Him by your complaining spirit, you cannot receive His divine comforts.

Your relationship with the mystical body of Christ, His church, is also hindered when your heart is plagued by discontentment. Burroughs concludes that murmuring and discontentment are below the high dignity bestowed by God on every believer.

Also, according to the Scriptures, murmuring and discontentment are evidence of an unbelieving heart. This murmuring state is what caused the children of Israel to lose their inheritance in the Promised Land. When they learned there were giants in the land, they "murmured against Moses and against Aaron" (Num. 14:2). They complained that it would

have been better to die in Egypt or in the wilderness than at
the hand of giants. And so they did.

They perished, in spite of the fact that God had promised
to fight with them and to give them their inheritance in the
Promised Land. He determined that because of their unbelief, expressed through their murmuring, they would not
enter into the inheritance He had prepared for them.

The New Testament warns believers against failing to
enter into the rest of God's redemption through unbelief, as
Israel did: "Take heed, brethren, lest there be in any of you
an evil heart of unbelief" (Heb. 3:12). We are admonished
to "labour therefore to enter into that rest, lest any man fall
after the same example of unbelief" (Heb. 4:11). The comforting promise is that "we which have believed do enter into
rest" (v. 3). Burroughs concludes:

> The spirit of every Christian should be like the spirit
> of his Father....We are one spirit with God, and with
> Christ, and one spirit with the Holy Ghost; there-
> fore we should have a spirit that might manifest the
> glorie [sic] of the Father, Son, and Holy Ghost in our
> spirits.... As Jesus Christ is the Lion of the tribe of
> Judah (so he is call'd), so we should manifest some-
> what of the lion-like spirit of Jesus Christ...in passing
> through all afflictions and troubles whatever without
> any murmuring against God.[26]

How to Attain the Jewel
of Contentment

Jeremiah Burroughs exclaims over believers who do not yet
enjoy their God: "You have abundance of mercies to bless
God for, but discontentedness makes them nothing. It's an

excellent speech that I remember Luther hath...the Spirit of God...makes all mercies seem to be great, and all afflictions seem to be little."[27]

Then he gives his parishioners practical instructions on how believers can attain to the promised state of divine rest:

1. Attend to your heart condition before God. Allow the grace and love of God to fill your heart and cleanse you of lesser things. Let your heart be mortified to the world so you can say with the apostle Paul, "I die daily" (1 Cor. 15:31).

2. Do not grasp too much of the world through personal greed. As the beloved apostle wrote, "If any man love the world, the love of the Father is not in him" (1 John 2:15).

3. Be sure of your call to every business you go about. Quiet your heart with this: "I know I am where God would have me. I am about the work that God has set me." Oh, this will quiet and content you when you meet with trouble.

4. Exercise much faith; that is the way to contentedness. Strengthen your spiritual conviction, not only in the promises of God but also in God Himself—His attributes revealed in His Word.

5. Labor to be spiritually minded: "If ye then be risen with Christ, seek those things which are above, where Christ sitteth on the right hand

of God. Set your affection on things above, not on things on the earth" (Col. 3:1–2).

6. Don't set high expectations for an exalted, extravagant way of life. As the apostle Paul asserted, "But godliness with contentment is great gain.... And having food and raiment let us be therewith content" (1 Tim. 6:6, 8). Remember your true source of contentment is the mystery of communion with God Himself.

7. Do not let the opinions of others affect your personal contentment. Their values cannot become "lords" over your pursuit of godly contentment.[28]

Finally, this godly pastor exhorted his parishioners:

> Oh! the Word holds forth a way full of comfort and peace to the people of God even in this world, you may live happy that lives in the midst of all the storms and tempests in the world, there is an Ark that you may come into, and no men in the world may live such comfortable, cheerfull, and contented lives as the saints of God.... O be not content with your selves till you have learned this lesson of Christian contentment, gotten some better skill in it than heretofore.[29]

It is obvious that Fanny Crosby learned the wonder of this mystery of divine contentment. As a result, she touched thousands of lives with her cheerful, loving demeanor. Her heart was filled with songs of praise to her lovely Savior, who held her affections throughout her ninety-plus years on this earth. How many saints over the centuries are still receiving comfort from her hymns that boldly declare her faith in God?

Fanny truly knew the reality of resting in His redemption, as is evident in one of her most beloved hymns:

> Redeemed, how I love to proclaim it!
> Redeemed by the blood of the Lamb;
> Redeemed through His infinite mercy,
> His child and forever I am.
>
> Redeemed, redeemed,
> Redeemed by the blood of the Lamb;
> Redeemed, redeemed,
> His child and forever I am.
>
> Redeemed, and so happy in Jesus,
> No language my rapture can tell;
> I know that the light of His presence
> With me doth continually dwell.
>
> I think of my blessed Redeemer,
> I think of Him all the day long:
> I sing, for I cannot be silent;
> His love is the theme of my song.
>
> I know there's a crown that is waiting,
> In yonder bright mansion for me,
> And soon, with the spirits made perfect,
> At home with the Lord I shall be.[30]

Personal Meditation

Chapter 7

Was Fanny Crosby content with who she was?

_____

_____

As we look at people like Fanny Crosby, do we think we have more peace than they do? Do they have greater peace in spite of their "limitations"?

_____

_____

Is Philippians 4:11–12 a request or a commandment that we be content?

_____

_____

Why does Jeremiah Burroughs call contentment a "rare jewel" in the Christian fellowship?

_____

_____

Has the lack of true Christian contentment been a constant struggle with mankind?

_____

_____

If we are resting in God's redemption, which fills us with contentment, would we be fulfilling the last commandment, "Thou shalt not covet"? In other words, will we have a desire to covet or otherwise violate the commandments of God as long as we are resting in His redemption?

_____

_____

Why is murmuring the opposite of contentment?

_____

_____

Do we have to have the mystery of enjoyment of God's sweet gifts?

_____

_____

Does our discontentment have undesirable consequences?

_____

_____

What are seven things Jeremiah Burroughs suggests we do to obtain contentment in Christ?

_____

_____

If we desire to properly acquaint ourselves with God and be at peace, we must know Him as He has revealed Himself…in the plurality of His persons. "God said, 'Let us make man in our image'" (Gen. 1:26). Do not let man be content until he knows something of the "us" from whom his being is derived.

—CHARLES SPURGEON[1]

8

Cultivating an Eternal Focus

WITH THE PROMISES of God available to every believer for living a life of peace, rest, and joy, it begs the question: *Why don't more Christians discover this "rare jewel" of Christian contentment?* What hinders them from triumphing in all of life's circumstances and from enjoying the mystery of romance with God Himself?

Richard Baxter, a British Reformed theologian of the 1600s, pointed out that the greatest obstacle to redemption for many people is the space between their head and their heart. Intellectually, they know the doctrines of Christ and their theology are correct, but they do not focus their hearts and minds on the eternal realities Christ came to reveal.[2]

Therefore, they fail to appropriate those profound truths to their everyday situations. So the knowledge of "us," to which Charles Spurgeon referred, eludes them. The truths of God's Word remain simply theory and not the transforming reality they were meant to be. As a result, these individuals never truly enter into fellowship and the mystery of the divine romance with their Redeemer. They are like the Jews to whom Jesus said:

> And ye have not [the Father's] word abiding in you:
> for whom he hath sent, him ye believe not. Search the
> scriptures; for in them ye think ye have eternal life: and
> they are they which testify of me. And ye will not come
> to me, that ye might have life.
>
> —JOHN 5:38–40

As you know, coming to Jesus is the first step to finding
contentment in life. The apostle John referred to Christ as the
Word: "In the beginning was the Word, and the Word was
with God, and the Word was God"
(John 1:1). All of Scripture points to
Christ as the Savior of the world, the
living Word of God. To refuse to come
to Him and to pursue a life of dependence upon Him results in a failure to
find life. Jesus said, "I am the way, the
truth, and the life: no man cometh
unto the Father, but by me" (John 14:6).

> **TO BE A
> VICTORIOUS
> CHRISTIAN,
> WE MUST
> FOCUS OUR
> LIVES ON
> ETERNAL
> VALUES.**

Only as we pursue by faith a life of
resting in His redemption will we adjust our focus to eternal
realities. To do that, we must recognize and set aside every
distraction that would keep us from abiding in Christ.

PUT AWAY DISTRACTIONS

Burroughs instructs the believer to labor to be spiritually
minded and to meditate often on things that are above. He
wrote, "Exercise faith by often resigning yourself to God, by
giving yourself up to God and His ways. The more you…sur-
render up yourself to God, the more quiet and peace you
will have."[3] He echoes the command of Scripture to seek

things that are above, where Christ is sitting at the right hand of God (Col. 3:1).

As we discuss specific distractions that hinder your faith, I invite you to identify any that might be preventing your focus on eternal values. I encourage you to courageously confront them in faith. By surrendering yourself completely to God in faith, you can overcome any distraction that would keep you from resting in His redemption. Oswald Chambers said: "Faith never knows where it is being led, but it loves and knows the One Who is leading."[4]

To be delivered from "wilderness wanderings" that threaten to defeat our pursuit of the mystery of divine romance, we need to repent of anything that is hindering our focus on eternal values. Tolerating attitudes and a lifestyle that do not correspond to what God's Word teaches is in itself a deadly distraction from the pursuit of relationship with God.

Sins we tolerate

Jerry Bridges is a naval officer who found Christ during his service in the military. Later, he became an executive with the Navigators, an organization dedicated to reaching men and women for Christ. He has written a book called *Respectable Sins: Confronting the Sins We Tolerate*. In it, Mr. Bridges lists twelve "respectable" sins that become distractions to resting in God's redemption. I have listed those sins below and added some commentary. As you consider each one, ask the Holy Spirit to show you if any of these are hindering your walk with God.

1. Ungodliness—a mind-set that is not focused on God or oriented toward Him

2. Anxiety and frustration—both of which block us from resting in God's redemption

3. Discontentment—often over situations that cannot be changed

4. Unthankfulness—not being appreciative for all the signs of God's goodness and tokens of His love that are brought into our lives every day

5. Pride—being focused on our way or our view, exalting ourselves so we don't rest in Him or surrender to Him so we can rest

6. Selfishness—a life focused on "me first," always asking, "How does this affect me? What can I get out of it?" Certainly this is the opposite of resting in His redemption.

7. Lack of self-control—not being willing to resist the devil and submit to God or say no and stand against dead-end roads that hinder us from walking with God

8. Impatience and irritability—which lead in the opposite direction from resting in His redemption. We want things to be convenient and we want things now, instead of resting and waiting on the Lord as Psalm 37:7 teaches: "Rest in the LORD, and wait patiently for him."

9. Anger—this is certainly the opposite of and an obstacle to resting in His redemption. Something displeases us and we respond with harshness, coldness, and withdrawal. These angry responses show our hearts are not resting in Him. We need to surrender to God, casting our burdens on Him, knowing that pleasing Him is what counts as we declare, "Thy will be done."

10. Judgmentalism—these attitudes hinder us from resting in His redemption. Having a critical spirit, fault-finding, nitpicking, and holding unwarranted bias against others certainly reflects a spirit that is not resting in God's redemption.

11. Envy and jealousy—these are reflected in not wanting others to have good things or be esteemed because we want those things for ourselves. This uncharitable attitude is a result of not finding our all in all in our Redeemer and resting in Him as the source of our joy and our contentment.

12. Worldliness—not completely withdrawing from modern society but learning to use this world and not abuse it (1 Cor. 7:31). Even good desires may go beyond their bounds and become obsessive, causing us to live for the creation and not the Creator, loving His gifts but denying the Giver.[5]

Unless we identify these "respectable" sins that we tolerate in our lives and repent from them, we will be hindered in our fellowship with Christ. Tolerating respectable sins, which God does not tolerate, blocks our communion with Him. Listen to the lament of the prophet Isaiah:

> Behold, the LORD's hand is not shortened, that it cannot save; neither his ear heavy, that it cannot hear: but your iniquities have separated between you and your God, and your sins have hid his face from you, that he will not hear.
>
> —ISAIAH 59:1–2

Independence

When we do not focus on eternal values, it is a sign that we are living *independently*, apart from the love and grace of the Redeemer. Independence, which is at the root of all sin, will distract us from fulfilling our God-given purpose. As we have discussed, it is our utter dependence and abandonment to Christ that lead us into the rest of God. That is what Christ is requiring of us when He asks us to deny ourselves, take up our cross, and follow Him (Matt. 16:24).

INDEPENDENCE, WHICH IS THE ROOT OF SIN, WILL DISTRACT US FROM FULFILLING OUR GOD-GIVEN PURPOSE.

Dependence on God means we are resting in Him and that we can do nothing without Him. *Independence* means we are on our own; we have our own agenda. We go our merry way, do our own thing, and leave God and others out of it. Dependence brings us into the family of God and lets us relate properly to the body of Christ as His children; independence makes us orphans, removed from the loving care of our Heavenly Father.

Jean-Pierre de Caussade declared: "In reality, holiness consists of one thing only: complete loyalty to God's will."[6]

In the introduction to his book, his translator quoted St. Albert the Great, who urged all Christians:

> Commit every particle of your being in all things, down to the smallest details of your life, eagerly and with perfect trust to the unfailing and most sure providence of God.[7]

When we commit our lives to the Spirit of God, we acknowledge that we cannot do anything without His love, His grace, or His Person. He becomes the consummation of our life. As a result of being totally dependent upon Him, our lives are filled with His peace and joy, and we rest in His redemption alone.

The apostle Jude instructs believers to "keep [themselves] in the love of God, looking for the mercy of our Lord Jesus Christ unto eternal life" (Jude 21). That is the work of faith: to consummate our life in the pursuit of God.

What does complete dependence look like in the life of a believer? B. B. Warfield describes it in the following paraphrased summary:

> The moralist must hold his breath and keep his muscles tense; and things go well with him only when he can do so. The truly religious man, on the contrary, finds his consolation in his very powerlessness; his trust is not in himself, but in his God; and the hour of his moral death turns into his spiritual birthday. The psychological analyst has caught the exact distinction

between moralism and religion. It is the distinction between trust in ourselves and trust in God.

The essence of faith, then, is the recognition of its utter helplessness, recognizing God as all in all in this most basic perception as to my ability, my lack, my want. In that, I review my sins and sense God's authority; I ask forgiveness and bow to His duties upon me.

Then I understand that faith is not first of all a positive quality, but the recognition of emptiness and a willingness to accept it as my true nature. It is a receptivity to hear God's voice and allow Him to fill this void. When I heard my Father's voice crying to me, my heart bounded in recognition. Without that response of faith, my soul was curiously dead and empty. I listen to the Divine Savior God calling, "Come unto me and I will give you rest" (Matt. 11:28).

It is as if the Savior is saying: "I am content to receive you; I rest in the atoning mercy for the legal dealing with sin; I rest in My love that provided it. I delight in mercy; I delight to dwell with you; I am satisfied with the relationship I will open to you, where you are nothing and I am everything. I am satisfied with that. And when you are satisfied with it, you will find rest in My rest."[8]

Lack of submission

Closely related to the distraction of an independent nature is a blatant lack of submission, which we described earlier as defiance. Because of our independence, we refuse to submit to the lordship of Christ. Yet enjoying a life of resting in His redemption requires complete submission to our Lord.

The idea of submission is foreign to most of us; we want to be in control and manage every aspect of our lives. This rebellion against the authority of Christ in our lives results in many difficulties. The Scriptures teach that "the way of the transgressors is hard" (Prov. 13:15). Yet sometimes, even unwittingly, many in our world today have chosen to walk in their own way without seeking God's blessing for their lives.

Social sanity has been lost in many ways because of rebellion—resulting, for example, in the use of illicit drugs and their destructive influence on all levels of culture. Cities that were once safe are safe no longer. Neighborhoods and communities, once open and caring, now cower behind locked doors and barred windows. In contrast, proper submission to and compliance with sane and civil norms of behavior, required by our legal authorities, result in stable environments, strong relationships, and peace in our culture.

In that same way, our submission to Christ removes the destructive influences from our lives that make life so hard. Only as we learn to become truly submissive to the Lord Jesus can we truly rest in His redemption and be cleansed of our rebellious heart. It is beautiful to behold a life that has truly bowed its will to the lordship of Christ.

SOCIAL SANITY HAS BEEN LOST IN MANY WAYS BECAUSE OF REBELLION.

Recently, when our family vacationed in Colorado, my grandson went horseback riding. When he mounted the horse he was to ride, it bowed down on its front knees to show its submission to my eight-year-old grandson. What a beautiful expression of submission! This noble creature had learned to accept its servant role to the master rider, even though that master was a child. In that same way, we must accept our servanthood and bow in submission to

Christ in order to find the true peace and joy He came to give us.

Ingratitude

In Jerry Bridges' list of respectable sins, he includes *unthankfulness*. Ingratitude is a first cousin to discontentment. It is characterized by a terrible lack of appreciation for the blessings we enjoy every day.

I personally believe that our greatest sin of commission is worry and that our greatest sin of omission is ingratitude. In her book *Radical Gratitude*, Ellen Vaughn discusses the power of gratitude:

> Radical gratitude is powerful, provocative, life-changing. It's like a pair of glasses that get progressively sharper: the more we thank, the more we see to be thankful for. Gratitude is the lens that reveals God's incredible grace at work. It is the key to tangible, everyday joy.[9]

Joy is really an expression of love and gratitude, which cannot be experienced in the emotional climate of unthankfulness. The Bible warns that in the last days, "men shall be lovers of their own selves, covetous, boasters, proud, blasphemers, disobedient to parents, unthankful, unholy" (2 Tim. 3:2), among other things.

INGRATITUDE IS A FIRST COUSIN TO DISCONTENTMENT.

The human heart is naturally ungrateful and always covets more than it has unless it submits to the lordship of Christ. In that place of humility, our eyes will be opened to the wonder of God's supernatural grace, and we will become forever grateful.

These sinful distractions must be displaced by the graces of God's love—pride for humility, covetousness for generosity, boastfulness for blessing others, ingratitude for gratitude, and unholiness for the true holiness that comes from God alone.

Becoming radically grateful is a powerful antidote for most sins that we consider "respectable." In truth, there is nothing respectable about sin. Only as we recognize it and ask the Holy Spirit to cleanse us can we be rid of the hindrances it causes to our resting in His redemption.

Worry

Worry has become so acceptable that it is almost considered a virtue by many. After all, it is noble to worry about your children, your spouse, the well-being of your friends, and even your community, isn't it? Worry is sometimes seen as a legitimate response to potential trouble; we have to figure out how to avoid the possible difficulty. It may sound good, except for one thing: Jesus taught us not to worry but to trust in Him.

As I mentioned, worry often accompanies unbelief. When we focus on trouble and allow ourselves to be filled with anxiety, we are not releasing faith in our loving Lord to provide the answer to our dilemma. We can't have it both ways: faith does not worry, and worry does not express faith.

In my book R_X *for Worry: A Thankful Heart,* I explain how being grateful and expressing our thanksgiving to God release our faith to believe Him for everything we need. Gratitude is the best medication for worry. As you dwell in an attitude of gratitude, you realize that as long as you are resting in His redemption, He is providing for you and you have nothing to worry about.

Medical science has concluded that many psychological diseases and physical conditions are a result of worry and negative mental attitude. If we truly believe, as Jesus promised, that He is our provider, we can live in a continual sense of peace, rest, and gratitude.

When you are tempted to doubt His goodness, I encourage you to read these words of Jesus:

> Therefore take no thought, saying, What shall we eat? or, What shall we drink? or, Wherewithal shall we be clothed?...for your heavenly Father knoweth that ye have need of all these things. But seek ye first the kingdom of God, and his righteousness; and all these things shall be added unto you.
> —MATTHEW 6:31, 32–33

"Seek ye first the kingdom of God." This priority of relationship with your Redeemer can set you free from your anxious outlook. I encourage you to talk to God in prayer.

WORRY HAS BECOME SO ACCEPTABLE THAT IT IS ALMOST CONSIDERED A VIRTUE BY MANY.

Tell Him how grateful you are for the price He paid for you to be restored to relationship with Him. Thank Him for creating you and for loving you so much that He would come to die for your sins to redeem you back to Himself.

I pray simply, "Lord, I thank You for the wonderful mystery of romance with You, which You ordained before the foundation of the earth. Thank You for Your love that longs to let me enjoy Your divine presence even while I am living here on earth."

Learning to commune with the Lord in these simple ways results in a powerful change of attitude and gives you a more positive approach to life. It sets you free from having to justify yourself and allows you to enjoy His peace and joy.

Trials of life

Learning to rest in God's redemption does not mean you will be exempt from painful situations. Facing the difficult challenges of life is precisely why you need to cultivate an intimate relationship with God. His supernatural grace will help you to endure life's hardships and perplexities without losing heart. Dr. Charles Stanley, in an article called "How Grace Changes Everything," explains:

> If you have been a believer for any length of time, you know that God doesn't always rescue us from painful situations. That's why we need sustaining grace. It upholds us, lifts us up, and strengthens us. If we walk in its power, you and I can face everything in life with confidence and assurance....
>
> Grace releases supernatural strength to keep us going despite our pain, suffering and loss....Grace ignites the determination to keep going no matter what. That is why some people never lose their joy and peace despite tremendous difficulty. Even in suffering, God's grace fills our lives with the fruit of the Spirit, such as strength, love, faith, kindness, and gentleness....
>
> No matter how difficult your circumstances become, your heavenly Father cares about you. He promises to take your suffering and bring something good from it.

> As you remain in close fellowship with the Lord, you
> will be able to tackle life's challenges with supernatural
> peace and joy. That's the power of sustaining grace.[10]

Without having cultivated intimate fellowship with the
Lord, many sincere believers give up when they face a painful
trial. Life circumstances become a distraction to their walk
with God because they have not learned to lean on Him, trust
Him, and rest in His love. It is impossible to live life without
facing difficult situations. But it is possible to face them with
the strength that comes from the supernatural grace of God
flowing through our lives.

Legalism

There is another, perhaps more subtle, distraction to
resting in His redemption that often poses as righteous
living—that is, *legalism*. Legalism is a religious perspective
that involves earning your salvation through good works. It
is the opposite of receiving salvation by grace alone through
faith. Many believers are still confused by this legalistic
approach to salvation—performing good deeds, living by
rules, and fulfilling men's traditions appeal to natural-
minded individuals who want to "save" themselves.

An entire book in the New Testament was written to
correct this error of legalism. The apostle Paul wrote to the
church at Galatia warning them not to turn away from faith
in Christ to "another gospel." It is believed by many students
of the Bible that the Galatians were a French tribe that settled
in 300 B.C. in the territory we now call Turkey. This letter is
the only one Paul wrote that did not encourage or commend
the people to whom he was writing.

Instead, Paul corrected the Galatians because they had

turned from receiving salvation through Christ by faith. They were reverting back to do the works of the law to earn their salvation. They did not place their trust in Christ's ultimate sacrifice in His death at Calvary. Listen to the apostle's stern rebuke:

> O foolish Galatians, who hath bewitched you, that ye should not obey the truth, before whose eyes Jesus Christ hath been evidently set forth, crucified among you?…Received ye the Spirit by the works of the law, or by the hearing of faith?
>
> —GALATIANS 3:1–2

Later in the letter, Paul lists their wrongdoing and then contrasts it with the fruit of the Spirit: "love, joy, peace, longsuffering, gentleness, goodness, faith, meekness, temperance" (Gal. 5:22–23). The only way we can emulate the godly fruit of the Spirit in our lives is to rest in the power of God's redemption.

> LEARNING TO REST IN GOD'S REDEMPTION DOES NOT MEAN YOU WILL BE EXEMPT FROM PAINFUL SITUATIONS.

There are many other distractions that can derail your godly pursuit of enjoying God and glorifying Him in all you do. As you search your heart, the Holy Spirit will be faithful to reveal anything in your life that is hindering your ultimate fulfillment in Christ. When you submit to His lordship in that area of your life, He will become your righteousness, peace, and joy.

Anticipating Heavenly Realities

One way to focus on eternal realities is to study the biblical promises for our future salvation in heaven with Him. David Jeremiah, pastor and prolific author, says there are five hundred references in the Scriptures to the place called *heaven*. The Scriptures teach that heaven is a literal place where God dwells and where Christ ascended after His resurrection, taking the righteous dead from paradise to be with Him.

> **LEGALISM IS A RELIGIOUS PERSPECTIVE THAT INVOLVES EARNING YOUR SALVATION THROUGH GOOD WORKS.**

When we learn to pursue a life of resting in God's redemption, it is natural to desire an eternal future with Him where He is—in heaven. In his book *The Saints' Everlasting Rest*, Richard Baxter states that he takes a walk in heaven every day. As he communes with God, he is filled with the anticipation of heaven and is filled with the heavenly quality of life we enjoy here when we are in His presence.[11]

There is a great similarity in our life of resting in God's redemption *now* and the *future* hope we have of living with Him forever in heaven. That is because the intimate relationship we share will only be greatly enhanced when we are transferred to our heavenly home to forever be with Christ. We enjoy the same mystery of consummation of divine romance here with our Lord as we will enjoy in heaven.

This parallel of heavenly realities is what the apostle Paul referred to when he wrote:

> If ye then be risen with Christ, seek those things
> which are above, where Christ sitteth on the right
> hand of God. Set your affection on things above, not
> on things on the earth. For ye are dead, and your life
> is hid with Christ in God. When Christ, who is our
> life, shall appear, then shall ye also appear with him
> in glory.
>
> —COLOSSIANS 3:1–4

When we "seek those things which are above," we learn to truly rest in His redemption and we experience a taste of the heavenly. The Bible says that this grace was given to us before the beginning of time:

> This grace was given us in Christ Jesus before the
> beginning of time, but it has now been revealed
> through the appearing of our Savior, Christ Jesus, who
> has destroyed death and has brought life and immor-
> tality to light through the gospel.
>
> —2 TIMOTHY 1:9–10, NIV

The love of God transcends time—past, present, and future—in giving to us the wonderful covenant of divine relationship, which is eternal. This never-ending love that comes to us from heaven is ours to enjoy on earth as we live our lives in Christ. To walk with Jesus here, to dwell in His presence and lean upon His bosom is a foretaste of heaven.

Even the Old Testament promises "days of heaven on the earth" for those who seek God:

> Therefore shall ye lay up these my words in your heart
> and in your soul, and bind them for a sign upon your
> hand....And ye shall teach them your children....And
> thou shalt write them upon the door posts of thine

> house, and upon thy gates: that your days may be multiplied, and the days of your children, in the land which the LORD sware unto your father to give them, *as the days of heaven upon the earth.*
>
> —DEUTERONOMY 11:18, 19, 20–21, EMPHASIS ADDED

The same requirement that Old Testament saints were given applies to New Testament believers: that we learn to abide in the Word of God in order that our days might be as days of heaven on the earth. Christ is the Word (John 1:1), and He taught us to abide in Him. When we set our affections on Him and make the priority of our lives to rest in His redemption, He will bring heaven to earth with His blessing on our lives.

Scripture teaches that heaven is a place where the saints worship unceasingly. Both Old and New Testaments express this joy of resting in His love here on earth:

> Thou wilt shew me the path of life: in thy presence is fulness of joy; at thy right hand there are pleasures for evermore.
>
> —PSALM 16:11

> One thing have I desired of the LORD, that will I seek after; that I may dwell in the house of the LORD all the days of my life, to behold the beauty of the LORD, and to enquire in his temple. For in the time of trouble he shall hide me in his pavilion: in the secret of his tabernacle shall he hide me.
>
> —PSALM 27:4–5

> Rejoice in the Lord always; again I will say, rejoice! Let your gentle spirit be known to all men. The Lord is near. Be anxious for nothing, but in everything by prayer and supplication with thanksgiving let your

requests be made known to God. And the peace of God, which surpasses all comprehension, will guard your hearts and your minds in Christ Jesus.

—PHILIPPIANS 4:4–7, NAS

There is no more joyous hope described in the Bible than the hope of seeing the face of our Lord. The beloved disciple, John, was granted that privilege as he received the book of the Revelation while in exile on the isle of Patmos. He could scarcely find words to describe the Christ whom He saw seated at the right hand of God in heaven.

We might think we would like to go back in time to walk with Christ by the Sea of Galilee, as the disciples did. We might dream of having lived when He taught the multitudes and healed the sick. What if we could have felt His hand on our shoulder and looked into His loving eyes?

But none of that could possibly compare to the time when we will see Him in the glory of heaven, entering into eternity with Him for all eternity. There, we will forever enjoy the Sabbath rest of God.

ENJOYING ETERNAL FRIENDSHIP WITH GOD

Henry David Thoreau said of true friendship:

> The most I can do for my friend is simply to be his friend. I have no wealth to bestow on him. If he knows that I am happy in loving him, he will want no other reward. Is not friendship divine in this?[12]

And Ralph Waldo Emerson concluded:

> A friend may well be reckoned the masterpiece of nature.[13]

Though Emerson was speaking of human friendship, he seems to have glimpsed something of what believers experience as the crown jewel of eternal friendship with God. When we choose to rest in His redemption, our divine friendship with God becomes the ultimate priority and passionate pursuit of our lives.

Resting in His redemption involves the consummation of all our mental activities. It transforms the ultimate expression of our convictions. Pursuing this divine rest motivates us to love, reason, and abandon in a way that involves us in the divine mystery of romance with God. He responds in love to our abandoned interaction with Him. This divine friendship with God exceeds the greatest love we have ever experienced. If we are truly resting in God's redemption, we are enjoying the most profound friendship available to man.

"MIRAGES" OF LIFE

Anything less than the pursuit of divine romance with God is a "mirage" of life, something that appears to be real but isn't. People seek the gratification of the moment offered by the mirage, regardless of the consequences.

> ANYTHING LESS THAN PURSUIT OF DIVINE ROMANCE WITH GOD IS A "MIRAGE" OF LIFE.

There is the mirage of *false ethics*, redefining morality and cultural standards according to our own design rather than the truth God presents in His Word. The mirage of *self-worship* deludes many into feeling entitled to get what they want regardless of the pain and injustice it inflicts on others. The mirage of *envy and jealousy* causes unhealthy competition and hatred for one who has something you want. Many times this mirage leads to murder, theft, and other forms of violence against humanity.

Solomon, the wisest man who ever lived, was also the wealthiest. God blessed him in his youth when he sought to know the wisdom of God as his priority in life. But Solomon left that place of solemn consecration and began to seek for life in many earthly pleasures. Only after he had tried everything and become disillusioned with life itself did he realize that God truly was the only reality and priority of life that mattered:

> Remember now thy Creator in the days of thy youth, while the evil days come not, nor the years draw nigh, when thou shalt say, I have no pleasure in them.... Let us hear the conclusion of the whole matter: Fear God, and keep his commandments: for this is the whole duty of man. For God shall bring every work into judgment, with every secret thing, whether it be good, or whether it be evil.
>
> —ECCLESIASTES 12:1, 13–14

In the end, Solomon realized that we were made to enjoy God and to glorify Him in all we do. When we set our minds to seek relationship with the one true God who can heal us, care for us, plan everything for the fulfillment of our destiny, and make our days like days of heaven on earth, we are learning to rest in His redemption.

And when we repent of our sins of commission and omission to receive His total forgiveness and be empowered to forgive others, the mystery of that divine romance becomes ours to enjoy. When we choose to abandon our worries and cares and submit ourselves to this divine covenant of love, we have entered into the mystery of eternal life in Christ.

This is true Christianity. Only when we have completely abandoned ourselves to His great redemption, making it our priority in living and our hope in dying, have we truly begun to enjoy what it means to be a Christian. Being a disciple of Christ is all about submitting our entire life to God's love and redemption. It is about resting in the pool of His grace, living in the river of His love, and enjoying a life without turmoil, cares, or anxiety. It is enjoying the assurance of our eternal salvation as well as temporal well-being in Christ alone.

When life seems dark and filled with hurt, loss, anxiety, and uncertainty, we need to make our friendship with God more secure. Helen Keller, who overcame deafness and blindness to learn to speak several languages, said, "Walking with a friend in the dark is better than walking alone in the light."[14]

> **WALKING WITH A FRIEND IN THE DARK IS BETTER THAN WALKING ALONE IN THE LIGHT.**
>
> —HELEN KELLER

Maintaining our focus on eternal friendship with Christ, who said He would be with us always, even to the end of the world (Matt. 28:20), is the perseverance of faith we need to be victorious in life.

If we temporarily lose this focus on our eternal friendship, it is important to recognize our dangerous plight and turn back to Christ alone. When we allow distractions, lack of fervency, and our own unfaithfulness to divert our attention, we must repent. In faith, we need to receive Christ's forgiveness and cast our cares, our circumstances, and our personal weaknesses on Him once again.

God's purpose for our lives never fails. He wants us to live our lives in His loving purposes, resting totally in His redemption. He wants our lives to be an answer to His high priestly prayer:

> That they all may be one; as thou, Father, art in me, and I in thee, that they also may be one in us: that the world may believe that thou hast sent me.... I in them, and thou in me, that they may be made perfect in one; and that the world may know that thou has sent me, and hast loved them, as thou hast loved me.
>
> —John 17:21, 23

If you desire to live a life that enjoys God and glorifies Him in all you do, learning to live daily resting in His redemption, then I invite you to pray this prayer with me:

Dear Lord Jesus,

I ask You to help me place my faith in Your total redemption, to enjoy the consummation of peace, joy, happiness, and effectiveness in my life here on earth. Help me to seek You first and make Your will for me to rest in Your redemption the priority of my life. In that way I will know I am forgiven and will be empowered to forgive others. I will learn to be content with You alone and will know the fulfillment for which I was designed by Your sovereign love. Thank You for hearing my prayer. As I choose to abide in Your Word, please make my days as days of heaven upon earth. And give me the wonderful hope of eternal bliss with You in heaven.

Amen.

Now, fellow pilgrim, begin (or continue) to enjoy the greatest journey on earth that guides you continually into the loving, eternal arms of God!

PERSONAL MEDITATION

CHAPTER 8

Richard Baxter believes we have a hard time getting our theological thoughts to move from our head to our hearts. What did he mean by that?

_____

_____

Are the Scriptures written to give us a more abundant life as we live them out each day?

_____

_____

Is the phrase "Peace be with you" just a passing greeting or does it have deep meaning?

_____

_____

Jerry Bridges lists twelve "respectable sins" of which we are often guilty. What are they?

_____

_____

Is our independence and defiance an impairment to Christianity?

_____

_____

Can we be such moralists that we can't rest and relax and accept God's grace?

_____

_____

Are lack of submission and legalism factors that may prevent us from resting in God's redemption?

_____

_____

Is thankfulness an aspect of humility that helps us to rest in God's redemption?

_____

_____

Do the trials of life humble us so that we can experience God's grace in a more reasonable manner?

_____

_____

As we look forward to our eternal consummation with God, do we really rest more in His redemption?

_____

_____

When we think of our Lord, do we think of Him as the One who planned all, created all, was incarnated in the world in Jesus, imputed His righteousness to all who believe in Christ's sacrifice, and gave us the privilege of consummation with Christ that is the greatest relationship of all of life that offers us the most peace?

_____

_____

Is it important that our relationship with Christ be the source of great joy? (See Colossians 1:9-11.)

_____

_____

Is our eternal friendship with the Creator the greatest relationship available to us?

_____

_____

Can we achieve this eternal friendship without the mystery and romance of abandoning ourselves to His grace, His love, and His redemption?

_____

_____

NOTES

INTRODUCTION

1. "Westminster Shorter Catechism with Proof Texts," Center for Reformed Theology and Apologetics, http://www.reformed.org/documents/WSC.html (accessed February 25, 2010).

2. Oswald Chambers, *My Utmost for His Highest* (Grand Rapids, MI: Discovery House, 1935), August 28 entry, emphasis added.

3. Ibid., October 17 entry, emphasis added.

4. R. T. Kendall, *How to Forgive Ourselves Totally* (Lake Mary, FL: Charisma House, 2007), 17–32.

5. Jeremiah Burroughs, *The Rare Jewel of Christian Contentment* (n.p.: L. Sadler and R Beaumont, 1651), 3.

6. Jeremiah Burroughs, *The Rare Jewel of Christian Contentment* (Lafayette, IN: Sovereign Grace Publishers, Inc., 2001), back cover.

7. Burroughs, *The Rare Jewel of Christian Contentment* (1651), 19.

PART 1
THE BIBLICAL BASIS FOR ALL PRAYER IS RESTING IN HIS REDEMPTION

1. Chambers, *My Utmost for His Highest,* August 28 entry.

CHAPTER 1
CREATED FOR COMMUNION WITH GOD

1. E. M. Bounds, *Purpose in Prayer* (Chicago: Moody, 1980), 9–10.

2. Jean-Pierre de Caussade, *Abandonment to Divine Providence* (New York: Image Books, 1975), 48–49.

3. "Westminster Shorter Catechism with Proof Texts."

4. See Miguel de Molinos, *The Spiritual Guide*, Classics of Western Spirituality Series (Mahwah, NJ: Paulist Press, 2010).

5. Oswald Chambers, *If You Will Ask,* Oswald Chambers Library Series (Grand Rapids, MI: Discovery House Publishers, 1994).

6. *Merriam-Webster Online Dictionary,* s.v. "rest," http://www.merriam-webster.com/dictionary/rest (accessed November 28, 2009).

7. Ibid.

8. Dante Alighieri, *Divine Comedy* 3.3.85.

9. *Merriam-Webster Online Dictionary*, s.v. "hamartia," http://www.merriam-webster.com/dictionary/hamartia (accessed March 5, 2010).

10. Dennis Linn, Sheila Fabricant Linn, and Matthew Linn, *Sleeping With Bread: Holding What Gives You Life* (Mahwah, NJ: Paulist Press, 1995).

11. Saint Augustine, *Confessions* 1.1, 5–6.

12. Ibid., 1.1.

13. "My Redeemer" by Philip P. Bliss. Public domain.

14. *Strong's Exhaustive Concordance*, no. 7673, s.v. "*shabbath*."

15. *WordNet*, s.v. "redemption," http://wordnetweb.princeton.edu/perl/webwn?s=redemption (accessed March 8, 2011).

CHAPTER 2
RECEIVING GOD'S REDEMPTION

1. Brainy Quote, s.v. "Charles Spurgeon," http://www.brainyquote.com/quotes/authors/c/charles_spurgeon.html (accessed January 28, 2010).

2. Oswald Chambers, *Biblical Ethics* (Fort Washington, PA: Christian Literature Crusade, 1964), 80.

3. Oswald Chambers, *Disciples Indeed* (Fort Washington, PA: Christian Literature Crusade, 1960), 57.

4. *Strong's Exhaustive Concordance*, no. G2842, s.v. "*koinonia*."

5. Oswald Chambers, *The Highest Good* (Fort Washington, PA: Christian Literature Crusade, 1965), 120.

PART 2
THE BIBLICAL BASIS FOR ALL CHRISTIAN LIVING IS RESTING IN HIS REDEMPTION

1. Oswald Chambers, *Approved Unto God* (Fort Washington, PA: Christian Literature Crusade, 1946), 104.

CHAPTER 3
FAITH FOR REDEMPTION

1. Gary Carter, pastor of Tampa Reformed Baptist Church, written and offered in gratitude to God for the lessons learned from the trials and triumphs of the faith of God's widows.

2. James P. Gills and Tom Woodward, *Darwinism Under the Microscope: How Recent Scientific Evidence Points to Divine Design* (Lake Mary, FL: Charisma House, 2002), 57.

3. See James P. Gills, *Exceeding Gratitude for the Creator's Plan: Discover the Life-Changing Dynamic of Appreciation* (Lake Mary, FL: Creation House, 2007), Day 1.

4. Ibid.

5. William and Robert Chambers, *Book of Days: A Miscellany,* July 30 entry, as quoted by Hillman's Hyperlinked and Searchable Chambers' Book of Days, http://www.thebookofdays.com/months/july/30.htm (accessed June 26, 2010).

6. William Penn, *No Cross, No Crown,* as quoted by Bill Samuel, "William Penn," QuakerInfo.com, http://www.quakerinfo.com/quakpenn.shtml (accessed March 8, 2011).

7. Chambers, *Book of Days.*

8. Samuel, "William Penn."

9. de Caussade, *Abandonment to Divine Providence,* 64.

10. *Strong's Exhaustive Concordance,* no. G2282, s.v. "*thalpo.*"

11. Brainy Quote, s.v. "Mother Teresa," http://www.brainyquote.com/quotes/authors/m/mother_teresa_2.html (accessed March 5, 2010).

12. Ibid.

13. Tentmaker Quotes, s.v. "Prayer Quotes," http://www.tentmaker.org/Quotes/prayerquotes.htm (accessed March 8, 2011).

14. James P. Gills, R_x *for Worry: A Thankful Heart* (Lake Mary, FL: Creation House, 2007), 5.

15. *Strong's Exhaustive Concordance,* no. G5513, s.v. "*chilaros.*"

16. W. E. Vine, *Vine's Expository Dictionary of New Testament Words,* s.v. "lukewarm."

17. *Strong's Exhaustive Concordance,* no. G769, s.v. "*astheneia.*"

18. Gills, R_x *for Worry,* 3.

19. Ibid.

20. *Merriam-Webster Online Dictionary,* s.v. "theology," http://www.merriam-webster.com/dictionary/theology (accessed March 5, 2010).

21. Paul Johnson, pastoral mentoring ministry of Vision New England, as quoted by the Sandberg Leadership Center, http://seminary.ashland.edu/slc/slc-POE.html (accessed February 28, 2010).

22. Stevan Becker, "Effective Christian Leadership: Vocation vs. Occupation," Whole Life Stewardship Reflections from Urbana.org, http://www.urbana.org/whole-life-stewardship-reflections/

effective-christian-leadership-vocation-vs-occupation (accessed February 18, 2010).

23. Ibid.

24. Richard J. Leider and David D. Shapiro, *Something to Live For: Finding Your Way in the Second Half of Life* (San Francisco, CA: Berrett-Kohler, 2008).

Chapter 4
Walking in God's Forgiveness

1. Preach-the-gospel.com, "John Newton Quotes," comp. Thomas George, http://preach-the-gospel.com/John-Newton-Quotes.htm (accessed March 8, 2011).

2. Ibid.

3. Ibid.

4. David Jeremiah, *Captured by Grace: No One Is Beyond the Reach of a Loving God* (Nashville, TN: Thomas Nelson, 2006), 103.

5. Ibid., 104.

6. *Merriam-Webster Online Dictionary*, s.v. "forgive," http://www.merriam-webster.com/dictionary/forgive (accessed March 8, 2011).

7. Dr. Woodward is a research professor and department chair of the theology department of Trinity College of Florida and the Tampa extension of Dallas Theological Seminary. He is well known as a premier historian for the Intelligent Design movement. He authored *Doubts About Darwin* (Baker Books, 2007) and *Darwin Strikes Back* (2006). He also coauthored with Dr. Gills *Darwinism Under the Microscope* (Charisma House, 2002) and has written other compelling books.

8. Brainy Quote, s.v. "Mother Teresa," http://www.brainyquote.com/quotes/authors/m/mother_teresa_2.html (accessed March 5, 2010).

9. Oswald Chambers, *Run Today's Race* (Fort Washington, PA: Christian Literature Crusade, 1968), 40.

Part 3
The Biblical Basis for Total Forgiveness Is Resting in His Redemption

1. R. T. Kendall, *Total Forgiveness* (Lake Mary, FL: Charisma House, 2002), xxiii–xxiv.

CHAPTER 5
FORGIVING OTHERS

1 Corrie ten Boom with John and Elizabeth Sherrill, *The Hiding Place* (Old Tappan, NJ: fleming H. Revell Co., 1977), 238.

2. Kendall, *Total Forgiveness*, back cover.

3. Charles Colson and Nancy Pearcey, *How Now Shall We Live?* (Carol Stream, IL: Tyndale, 1999).

4. Kendall, *Total Forgiveness*, 11–19.

5. Ibid., 19–32.

6. Ibid., 4.

7. Kendall, *How to Forgive Ourselves Totally*, 175–176.

8. Ibid.

CHAPTER 6
FREEDOM FROM CONDEMNATION

1. Kendall, *Total Forgiveness*, 141.

2. Kendall, *How to Forgive Ourselves Totally*, 18.

3. Corrie ten Boom, *Tramp for the Lord* (New York: Jove, 1974), 53.

4. Kendall, *How to Forgive Ourselves Totally*, 190–192.

5. de Caussade, *Abandonment to Divine Providence*, 68–69.

6. David Powlison, "A Personal Liturgy of Confession," Christian Counseling and Educational Foundation, http://www.ccef.org/personal-liturgy-confession (accessed December 30, 2009).

PART 4
THE BIBLICAL BASIS FOR DIVINE CONTENTMENT IS RESTING IN HIS REDEMPTION

1. Burroughs, *The Rare Jewel of Christian Contentment* (2001), 1–2.

CHAPTER 7
DIVINE CONTENTMENT

1. Ed Hird, "Fanny Crosby: The World's Most Prolific Songbird," *Deep Cove Crier*, March 2006, http://www3.telus.net/st_simons/cr0603.html (accessed March 8, 2011).

2. "Saved by Grace" by Fanny Crosby. Public domain.

3. Fanny Crosby, *Fanny J. Crosby: An Autobiography* (Peabody, MA: Hendrickson, 2008), 24.

4. Ibid., 37.

5. Ibid., 105.

6. Sam Shin, "Lessons Grom a Blind Beggar," *Gospel Prism* (blog), February 15, 2011, http://www.wellspringsg.org/blogs/gospelprism/2011/02/15/lessons-from-a-blind-beggar/ (accessed March 12, 2011).

7. Fanny Crosby and Samuel Trevena Jackson, *Fanny Crosby's Story of Ninety-Four Years* (New York: Fleming Revell, 1915), 178.

8. Ed Hird, "Fanny Crosby: The World's Most Prolific Songbird," http://www3.telus.net/st_simons/cr0603.html (accessed March 12, 2011).

9. Burroughs, *The Rare Jewel of Christian Contentment* (2001), 12.

10. Burroughs, *The Rare Jewel of Christian Contentment* (1651), 50.

11. Saint Augustine, *Confessions* 1.1.

12. Burroughs, *The Rare Jewel of Christian Contentment* (2001), 14.

13. Ibid.

14. Ibid., 13.

15. Ibid., 14.

16. Burroughs, *The Rare Jewel of Christian Contentment* (1651), 24.

17. Burroughs, *The Rare Jewel of Christian Contentment* (2001), 18.

18. Burroughs, *The Rare Jewel of Christian Contentment* (1651), 28.

19. Ibid., 29–30.

20. Ibid., 45, 71.

21. Burroughs, *The Rare Jewel of Christian Contentment* (2001), 57.

22. Burroughs, *The Rare Jewel of Christian Contentment* (1651), 101.

23. Ibid., 84.

24. Ibid., 80.

25. Ibid., 85.

26. Ibid., 87–88.

27. Ibid., 92.

28. Burroughs, *The Rare Jewel of Christian Contentment* (2001), 93–95.

29. Burroughs, *The Rare Jewel of Christian Contentment* (1651), 140–141.

30. "Redeemed, How I Love to Proclaim It!" by Fanny Crosby. Public domain.

CHAPTER 8
CULTIVATING AN ETERNAL FOCUS

1. Charles Spurgeon, *Morning and Evening,* Revised Modern English Version (New Kensington, PA: Whitaker House, 2001), May 8 Evening entry.

2. Richard Baxter, *The Reformed Pastor* (Whitefish, MT: Kessinger, 2007).

3. Burroughs, *The Rare Jewel of Christian Contentment* (2001), 95.

4. Chambers, *My Utmost for His Highest,* March 19 entry.

5. Jerry Bridges, *Respectable Sins: Confronting the Sins We Tolerate* (Colorado Springs, CO: NavPress, 2007).

6. de Caussade, *Abandonment to Divine Providence,* 24.

7. Ibid., 17.

8. B. B. Warfield, "What Is Calvinism?" originally printed in *The Presbyterian,* March 2, 1904, http://qqohelet.tripod.com/bbw_calv .htm (accessed March 8, 2011).

9. Ellen Vaughn, *Radical Gratitude: Discovering Joy Through Everyday Thankfulness* (Grand Rapids, MI: Zondervan, 2005), back cover.

10. Charles Stanley, "How Grace Changes Everything, Part 4: Sustaining Grace," InTouch Ministries, Life Principles Notes, http:// intouch.org/Content/3/LP080316%20Grace%20Changes%20Pt%204 .pdf (accessed March 12, 2011).

11. Richard Baxter, *The Saints' Everlasting Rest* (Grand Rapids, MI: Christian Classics Ethereal Library, n.d.), 99–109, http:// newdemonstration.com/files/books/richard-baxter/Richard%20 Baxter%20-%20Saint's%20Everlasting%20Rest.pdf (accessed March 12, 2011).

12. Think Exist, s.v. "Henry David Thoreau," http://thinkexist .com/quotation/the_most_i_can_do_for_my_friend_is_simply_to_ be/7806.html (accessed March 8, 2011).

13. Brainy Quote, s.v. "Ralph Waldo Emerson," http://www
.brainyquote.com/quotes/authors/r/ralph_waldo_emerson.html
(accessed March 8, 2011).

14. Brainy Quote, s.v. "Helen Keller," http://www.brainyquote
.com/quotes/quotes/h/helenkelle384608.html (accessed March 8,
2011).

The Writings of James P. Gills, M.D.

A Biblical Economics Manifesto
(With Ron H. Nash, Ph.D.)
The best understanding of economics aligns with what the Bible teaches on the subject.
ISBN: 978-0-88419-871-0
E-book ISBN: 978-1-59979-925-4

Believe and Rejoice: Changed by Faith, Filled With Joy
Observe how faith in God can let us see His heart of joy.
ISBN: 978-1-59979-169-2
E-book ISBN: 978-1-61638-727-3

Come Unto Me: God's Call to Intimacy
Inspired by Dr. Gills' trip to Mt. Sinai, this book explores God's eternal desire for mankind to know Him intimately.
ISBN: 978-1-59185-214-8
E-book ISBN: 978-1-61638-728-0

Darwinism Under the Microscope: How Recent Scientific Evidence Points to Divine Design
(With Tom Woodward, PhD)
Behold the wonder of it all! The facts glorify our Intelligent Creator!
ISBN: 978-0-88419-925-0
E-book ISBN: 978-1-59979-882-0

The Dynamics of Worship
Designed to rekindle a passionate love for God, this book gives who, what, where, when, why, and how of worship
ISBN: 978-1-59185-657-3
E-book ISBN: 978-1-61638-725-9

Exceeding Gratitude for the Creator's Plan: Discover the Life-Changing Dynamic of Appreciation
Standing in awe of the creation and being secure in the knowledge of our heavenly hope, the thankful believer abounds in appreciation for the Creator's wondrous plan.
ISBN: 978-1-59979-155-5
E-book ISBN: 978-1-61638-729-7

God's Prescription for Healing: Five Divine Gifts of Healing
Explore the wonders of healing by design, now and forevermore.
ISBN: 978-1-59185-286-5
E-book ISBN: 978-1-61638-730-3

Imaginations: More Than You Think
Focusing our thoughts will help us grow closer to God.
ISBN: 978-1-59185-609-2
E-book ISBN: 978-1-59979-883-7

Love: Fulfilling the Ultimate Quest
Enjoy a quick refresher course on the meaning and method of God's great gift.
ISBN: 978-1-59979-235-4
E-book ISBN: 978-1-61638-731-7

Overcoming Spiritual Blindness
Jesus + anything = nothing. Jesus + nothing = everything. Here is a book that will help you recognize the many facets of spiritual blindness as you seek to fulfill the Lord's plan for your life.
ISBN: 978-1-59185-607-8
E-book ISBN: 978-1-59979-884-4

Resting in His Redemption
We were created for communion with God. Discover how to rest in His redemption and enjoy a life of divine peace.
ISBN: 978-1-61638-349-7
E-book ISBN: 978-1-61638-425-8

Rx for Worry: A Thankful Heart
Trust your future to the God who is in eternal control.
ISBN: 978-1-59979-090-9
E-book ISBN: 978-1-59979-926-1

The Prayerful Spirit: Passion for God, Compassion for People
Dr. Gills tells how prayer has changed his life as well as the lives of patients and other doctors. It will change your life also!
ISBN: 978-1-59185-215-5
E-book ISBN: 978-1-61638-732-7

The Unseen Essential: A Story for Our Troubled Times... Part One
This compelling, contemporary novel portrays one man's transformation through the power of God's love.
ISBN: 978-1-59185-810-2
E-book ISBN: 978-1-59979-513-3

Tender Journey: A Story for Our Troubled Times... Part Two
Be enriched by the popular sequel to *The Unseen Essential*.
ISBN: 978-1-59185-809-6
E-book ISBN: 978-1-59979-509-6